Hike the Bluegrass and Beyond

Your Guide to Hiking, Walking and Strolling Across Central Kentucky

D1599138

Earth laughs in flowers.

~Ralph Waldo Emerson, "Hamatreya"

Hike the Bluegrass and Beyond

Your Guide to Hiking, Walking and Strolling Across Central Kentucky

By
Valerie L. Askren

Hike the Bluegrass and Beyond
Your Guide to Hiking, Walking and Strolling
Across Central Kentucky

Published by 42nd Parallel, LLC, a tiny operation unbeknownst to most. We can be reached at hikethebluegrass@gmail.com.
If you insist on snail-mailing us, you can send any correspondence to
233 Kingsway Drive, Lexington, KY 40502.

All photos are by the author, with the exception of those taken by Kathy aka "The Cesspool of Knowledge" and Handsome Dave. They graciously allowed me to include them in this book, but retain all other rights to their photos. All maps are original and were created by the author with help from her cohorts, Kathy and Ben. Kathy also did the awesome layout design. Thanks everyone!

ISBN 978-0-692-54737-3
Revised Edition.
This book is an expansion of the original *Hike the Bluegrass*.

Front cover: Anglin Falls, John B. Stephenson Memorial Forest SNP
Back cover: Walt and Emma at Yahoo Creek

Acknowledgments

For fun.

And for all my friends...

Contents

Part 1: Hiking Trails

Part 2: Urban Walking Trails

Part 3: Gardens

Part 4: Natural Areas Stewardship

Part 5: You Must Choose...but Choose Wisely

Let's get out and do something!

How many times have you said that? You've been stuck at home or in the office for way too long. Your legs are itching for a work out. Your muddled head needs fresh air. The in-laws, the outlaws, the kids...they're all driving you crazy. So whether it's a heart-pumping hike up to a breath-taking overlook or a quiet stroll in a Japanese-inspired garden, this book has lots of ideas to help you get out and do something!

Not everyone has the time to hike the Appalachian Trail or climb K2. But that doesn't mean you have to spend every weekend on the couch. Most hikes in this book are less than 45 minutes from Lexington, and many are less than 30. And several could be done after work on those long dog days of summer. But don't confine your outdoor pursuits to the warmer months. Fall and winter can bring smaller crowds and fewer bugs. And even a light snowfall can create great opportunities for animal tracking or cause stalactites to form on your favorite waterfall.

Who is this book designed for?
For those new to the outdoors, nearly every hike in this book can be modified to meet your skill level. Are you new to the Bluegrass? Here is a great way to discover the beauty and rigors of Central Kentucky. Recently retired and finding yourself with more free time? Choose just one hike each week and it would take you over a year to work your way from cover to cover. Even veteran hikers will find many trails and walks they have not previously discovered in the region.

Young families with children and those with mobility challenges will appreciate the reference charts in the back of the book which identifies hikes suitable for all ages and abilities. Ditto for the dog lovers among us, as many locations are noted as pet-friendly.

What doesn't this book cover?
The scope of the book is limited to those hikes located in Central Kentucky, while not replicating many of the guidebooks already out there. Sample hikes are included for the Red River Gorge, the Big South Fork, and the Sheltowee Trace. But the primary focus of *Hike the Bluegrass and Beyond* is the multitude of hiking options that fewer people know about and that are closer to the Bluegrass region.

How is the book organized?
Part One of the book concentrates on non-paved hiking, whether it's a 13-mile trek or a half-mile nature trail. Included are over 50 hikes within the Bluegrass that many people have not heard of, but are soon to make your favorite short list.

Part Two focuses on urban walks on paved surfaces. These options may be more appealing during different times of the year or for different groups of people. Keep these walks in mind when you have guests in town for the weekend, conditions are muddy, or you want to push that new jogging stroller.

Part Three of the book describes a selection of gardens in the Bluegrass that are free and open to the public. Walking trails in this section include both paved and unpaved trails, but typically are shorter in duration than traditional hikes.

Part Four covers some of the rules and regulations governing Kentucky's scenic hiking areas. Please read through these pages and practice the Leave No Trace Principles included in the back of the book.

Part Five includes two charts you might find handy to help you narrow your choices when trying to select a hike for a particular outing. You may want to start here by identifying which trails meet your criteria for a particular hike on a given day. Information includes sorting options by trail length; distance from Lexington; the availability of paved trails, bathrooms, or visitor centers; and which locations are kid or pet-friendly.

Before starting out...
...always assume that you will be out longer than you planned. Begin with a good pair of hiking or walking shoes, a full water bottle, and a healthy snack. For longer hikes you might want to throw in a first-aid kit, bug repellent, compass (or smart phone), and some rain gear. And don't forget your smile and sense of adventure.

Finally, a word about maps.
All the trails in *Hike the Bluegrass and Beyond* were hiked by the author using a hand-held GPS device. Roads and waterways were then added using open- source mapping data. In many cases, maps for a given hike or park are also available on the Internet, including many with topographic features.

The maps in this book were designed to give you a general feel for the layout of the hike and are not for navigation purposes. On all maps, north is pointing up and trailheads are marked with a TH (white letters within a black circle). While all maps are to scale, the actual scale varies from map to map and is not included. That said, for most of the hikes covered in this book, the maps provided are more than sufficient for the average person to leave their vehicle and find it once again.

The opportunities for outdoor recreation in the Bluegrass keep growing. In the time it takes you to drive around New Circle Road during rush hour, you could be on a wild and scenic trail. So whether you bought this book, borrowed it from a friend, or simply used it for inspiration, get out and take a hike!

Hiking Trails

1 Asbury Trails at the Palisades Farm
2 Bark Camp Creek
3 Bee Rock and Rockcastle Narrows
4 Berea College Forest
5 Bernheim Arboretum
6 Blue Licks State Nature Preserve
7 Boone Station State Historic Site
8 Buckley Wildlife Sanctuary
9 Camp Nelson Civil War Heritage Park
10 Camp Wildcat Civil War Battlefield
11 Capitol View Park
12 Carter Caves State Park
13 Cave Run Lake: Caney Trail Loop
14 Cave Run Lake: Furnace Arch
15 Central Kentucky Wildlife Refuge
16 Civil War Fort at Boonesboro
17 Clay Wildlife Management Area
18 Cove Spring Park Nature Preserve
19 Crutcher Nature Preserve
20 Dog Slaughter Falls
21 Dupree Nature Preserve
22 Eagle Falls
23 Elkhorn Creek Nature Trail
24 Floracliff Nature Sanctuary
25 Griffith Woods WMA
26 Hisle Park
27 Jim Beam Nature Preserve
28 John A. Kleber WMA
29 John Stephenson Memorial Forest

30 Leslie Morris Park at Fort Hill
31 Lick Creek and Princess Falls
32 Lower Howard's Creek
33 Masterson Station Park
34 Maywoods
35 McConnell Springs
36 Natural Arch Scenic Area
37 Natural Bridge: Laurel Ridge Trail
38 Natural Bridge: Rock Garden Trail
39 Perryville Battlefield
40 Pilot Knob State Nature Preserve
41 Quiet Trails State Nature Preserve
42 Raven Run Nature Sanctuary
43 Red River Gorge: Auxier Ridge
44 Red River Gorge: Rock Bridge
45 Red River Gorge: Trailapalooza
46 Salato Wildlife Education Center
47 Sally Brown Nature Preserve
48 Shaker Village: The Nature Preserve
49 Skullbuster
50 Tom Dorman State Nature Preserve
51 Vanhook Falls
52 Veterans Memorial WMA
53 Veterans Park
54 War Fork Creek / Resurgence Cave
55 Waterfall Chasing: Jackson and Lee
56 Yahoo Falls and Yahoo Arch
57 Yahoo Loop via Negro Creek

Urban Gardens Location Map

73 The Arboretum: State Botanical Garden of Kentucky
74 Ashland: The Henry Clay Estate
75 Jack Jouett House Historic Site
76 Josephine Sculpture Park
77 Lexington Cemetery
78 Nannine Clay Wallis Arboretum
79 Scott County Native Plants Arboretum
80 Waveland State Historic Site
81 Woodland Park Tree Trail
82 Yuko-En on the Elkhorn and the Cardome Walking Trail

Part 1
Hiking Trails

Forget not that the earth delights
to feel your bare feet
and the winds long to play with your hair.
~Kahlil Gibran

1 Asbury Trails at the Palisades Farm

Best hiked in the spring for a spectacular show of wildflowers and waterfalls.

Trail Length: 2-3 miles

Facilities: No bathrooms or water available.

Hours: Open daily 8 am-8 pm (sunrise to sunset, from October to March).

Additional Information: Hiking is free and open to the public. Dogs are permitted, but should be on-leash. Trail maps and a self-guided brochure of interesting sites are available at the trailhead kiosk.

Directions: From Lexington, head south on Harrodsburg Road (US 68 W). From the intersection of Harrodsburg Road and Man O' War Boulevard, drive 9.2 miles. Continue straight on Lexington Road (KY 29, at the Shell Station) towards Wilmore (where US 68 W careens sharply to your right.) Stay on KY 29 (aka High Bridge Road) through downtown Wilmore. Drive 0.4 miles south of the Lowry Lane stop light, then turn right on Shanty Hill Lane. Drive another 0.7 miles until the road takes a sharp bend to the left. At the curve, turn right, go through the gates, and park in the gravel lot on your left. The trail kiosk can be seen from the parking lot.

Catch these trails after a good rain in early to late spring and you'll be rewarded with clouds of larkspur and phacelia; stonecrop nestled amongst the rocks; Solomon's seal of biblical proportion; and seldom-seen shooting stars. Though the creeks can run dry, several waterfalls tumble off the palisades towering above the Kentucky River. Located on lands owned by Asbury University, we are fortunate the school is so willing to share the beauty of the area.

Begin your hike at the trailhead kiosk, being sure to pick up a map and walking guide if you have not already printed one out. Just west of the kiosk, the trail splits in two. If you turn right, you will be on the Hillside Trail, which leads to the stone foundation of an old mill. Limited creek flows suggest that the mill only operated intermittently and probably ground corn for the families who lived nearby. Continuing on this half-mile trail takes you behind Asbury's equestrian facilities, forcing you to walk sandwiched between four-board fencing and the bluff overlooking the river. The views are occasionally worthwhile. If the horses have chewed up this section of the path, you may want to turn around at the old mill and retrace your steps.

A left at the trail split just west of the trailhead kiosk, leads you along the Old Stage Road Trail, which today is barely wide enough for a MINI Cooper. The trail descends about two-thirds of a mile to the Kentucky River. Unlike earlier travelers, no toll payments are necessary to cart your goods down to the remains of the old storehouse foundation. At low water levels, wagons could ford the river, enabling them to continue to Danville.

Soon after starting the trail, the Old Stage Road crosses a gravel road leading to a water pumping station. Cross the road and continue your descent along a wet-weather creek, frequently interrupted by small waterfalls and cascading slides. Celandine poppies, ferns, anemones, bloodroot, and large-leaved waterleaf abound. At the bottom of the hill, the trail reaches the banks of the river. Don't cross the bridge just yet——turn left (south) here to pick up the Great Wall Trail. On your left is the old storehouse foundation, comfortably surrounded by the glorious purple hues of larkspur in mid-spring and quietly guarded by huge Solomon's seal in late May.

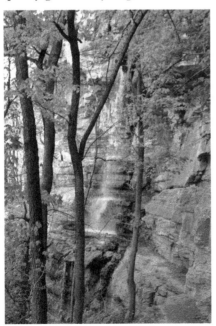

The Great Wall Trail runs about 0.25 miles (one-way), beneath 400-foot palisades overlooking the river. Take time to enjoy the first waterfall you come to on the trail. A well-marked path leads straight up to an interesting cave, spring, and rock formation at the top of the falls. If you find yourself daring of heart and strong of lungs, follow the path a short distance, stopping to admire the wildflowers as you catch your breath. Snap a few pictures and return back down the spur the same way you came up.

Continue along the Great Wall Trail as far as you can go. Several other waterfalls, most of which are spring-fed, tumble onto and over the path. If you're lucky enough to hike here in spring, columbine and shooting stars will add a touch of color and romance to your hike.

Once at the end of the trail, trace your steps back to the merger of the Old Stage Road and Great Wall trails. This time cross north on the wood bridge to the pump station. Follow the gravel road back up the hill to intersect with the hiking trails. Alternately, you can simply follow the Old Stage Road back to the kiosk. Either way, you may want to consider the value of tithing to support more natural areas such as this one.

Trail Map: https://goo.gl/jcIsZG

Side Trip:
If you're looking for a bite to eat you might want to try downtown Wilmore, including Solomon's Porch (111 E. Main Street); La Casa de Jose (325 E. Main Street); or Sims Old-Fashioned Soda Fountain and Grill (319 E. Main Street). After dinner consider a relaxing stroll around the impressive brick buildings that anchor the campus of Asbury University.

Asbury Trails at the Palisades Farm
Shanty Hill Lane
Wilmore, KY 40390
Phone: (859) 858-3511
**Web: www.asbury.edu/academics/departments/
natural-sciences/facilities/asbury-trails**

2 Bark Camp Creek

A classic streamside hike leading to the Bark Camp Creek cascades.

Trail Length: 5.2 miles, with more mileage readily available.

Facilities: None (and sometimes that's a good thing).

Hours: None posted.

Additional Information: Bark Camp Creek is stocked with rainbow and brown trout annually. Kentucky fishing regulations apply. Dogs can go off-leash.

Directions: From I-75 south, take exit #25 at Corbin. Turn right on US 25 W. Drive 4.7 miles. Turn right onto KY 1193. Drive another 4.6 miles. Stay straight on KY 1277 where KY 1193 bears to the right. (KY 1277 is known as Bee Creek Road on some maps, but is not physically marked as such.) Drive 1.2 miles. You will see a slightly misleading, brown Forest Service sign for FS 88 and State Hwy 90 on your right. *Immediately* past the sign, turn left onto Forest Service Road 193, a gravel road lightly pocked with potholes. In 1.7 miles the road will cross Bark Camp Creek. Shoulder parking is available on the right side of the road for 4-5 cars.

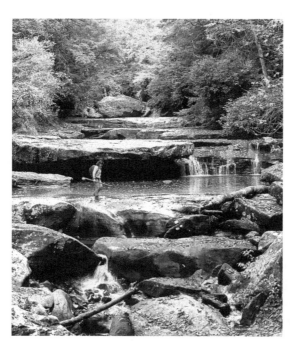

Canine lovers unite! Not only can you hike with Fido, but he doesn't need a trout permit to fish here (although you do). But seriously, the only thing not to like about this hike is you'll want more of it. Fortunately, the trail converges with several other opportunities.

FS 193 crosses Bark Camp Creek where the stocking truck releases rainbows and browns each year in months 3, 4, 5, 6 and 10. As you might suspect, this is a great place for locals to go for carry-out fish. So sometimes the trailhead gets a little trashed. But in no time the hike quickly turns almost pristine and what makes this creek great for trout, makes it great for hiking. The spring-fed waters stay cool and clear year-round, with towering hemlocks providing lots of soothing shade.

Bark Camp Trail #413 follows the creek as it flows west for 2.6 miles, passing under several rockhouses and through lush thickets of rhododendron and mountain laurel. About two miles from the trailhead, a new bridge has been built, re-routing the trail to the left (south) side of the creek. The old bridge, located further downstream, had washed out one time too many.

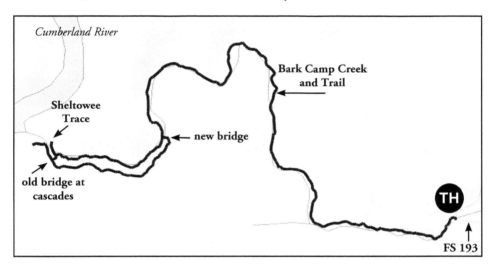

When you get to the new bridge, you have a few choices. To follow the Bark Camp Trail proper, cross the bridge and walk on the southern side (creek-left) of Bark Camp Creek. A half-mile later, the trail will merge with the Sheltowee Trace just below what is known as Bark Camp Creek cascades, and where the Sheltowee bears south following the Cumberland River. Following the Sheltowee a short distance will lead you to the Bark Camp Creek Shelter, available for an overnighter or a hot fire on a cold day. At this juncture, you could turn around and trace your steps back to the trailhead. Alternately, if you are looking for a little more mileage, hikers can turn south on this section of the Sheltowee Trace, also known as the Moonbow Trail, for a longer out-and-back hike.

If you do not cross the new bridge, technically you will be on the Sheltowee Trace, which will also take you to the cascades. The Trace will then bear north and follow the Cumberland River. However, look on your left for the steep trail leading to the creek. If water levels are low enough, you can make a small loop by carefully crossing Bark Camp Creek at the site of the old washed-out bridge. Then pick up Bark Camp Creek trail and head back upstream to the new bridge.

Another option would be to combine the Bark Camp Creek, Moonbow, and Dog Slaughter Creek trails (described elsewhere in this book), to form an 8.6-mile hike (requiring a shuttle) or an extended out-and-back, day hike.

Trail Maps:
A US Forest Service trail map can be found at: http://goo.gl/v2lcPV. Topo maps of the area can be found at Sheltowee Trace National Recreation Trail: http://goo.gl/BoRiJh (numbers 7 and 8 are the ones you'll want to use here.) An online, mobile-compatible map can also be found at outrageGIS mapping: http://goo.gl/KzbDmd.

Side Trip:
If all this hiking has made you hungry, check out the Wrigley Brewery and Taproom in Corbin. They have farm to table food, an incredible craft beer selection, and several bourbon offerings. Live music is frequently heard. Open Wednesday through Thursday, 5 pm-11 pm; Friday and Saturday 5 pm-12 pm. Find them at thewrigley.com or on FB; 207 S. Main Street, Corbin, KY 40701. (606) 261-2008.

US Forest Service - London District
761 S. Laurel Road
London, KY 40744
Phone: (606) 864-4163
Web: http://goo.gl/ira2yP

3 Bee Rock and the Rockcastle Narrows - West

The trail climbs to Bee Rock, a bluff overlooking the Rockcastle River, before descending back to the river, with an optional spur to Beech Creek.

Trail Length: 5.4 miles; 7.0 miles with the optional spur.
Facilities: Campground, bathrooms and water (seasonally available).
Hours: None posted.
Additional Information: The fishing is good and dogs can go off-leash.
Directions: From I-75, take exit #38 for London. Turn right (west) on KY 192. Travel 18 miles. Just before crossing the Rockcastle River, turn right into the Bee Rock Picnic Area and Campground (FS 624). Park near Sublimity Bridge, on the south (Laurel County) side of the river.

This hike combines the Bee Rock Loop Trail #529 and the Rockcastle Narrows Trail #503 to form a 5.4-mile loop. To begin the hike, walk over Sublimity Bridge (closed to vehicular traffic) until you're on the north (Pulaski County) side of the river. Built by the Civilian Conservation Corp in the 1930s, the rock foundation of Sublimity Bridge is a beautiful piece of work. Once across the bridge, turn left (west) and walk the paved road for about 0.25 miles, until you see the trailhead on your right.

Whoa. Back up. Did you say Sublimity Bridge? Maybe before we begin hiking we should start with a short story. In the mid-1800s, the Rockcastle River was the site of several resort hotels that attracted visitors from hundreds of miles around with claims of medicinal springs, fine dining, comfortable lodging, and enticing entertainment. The largest and best known of these was the Rockcastle Springs Resort Hotel, located about seven miles downstream of here, at the confluence of the Rockcastle and Cumberland rivers.

Around 1850, Dr. Christopher Columbus 'C.C.' Graham built another resort on the Pulaski County side of what is now Bee Rock Campground, known as the Sublimity Springs Resort Hotel. In addition to the hotel, Dr. Graham built slave quarters, horse stables, a gristmill, and a sawmill along the river. (Dr. Graham has mistakenly been credited with creating graham flour, but we truly digress.) The resort, which operated for about 30 years, charged a daily rate of 75 cents or $5 per week.

About a mile upriver from the Sublimity Bridge, the Warner Hotel stood at the confluence of the Rockcastle River and Cane Creek. A two-story structure, built entirely of chestnut wood, the hotel operated until the early 1900s. Scant evidence of the hotel's remains can be seen along the Rockcastle Narrows East Trail (#401) on the Laurel County side of the river.

Beach Narrows Trail

Bee Rock
Loop Trail

Rockcastle Narrows Trail

Bee Rock Overlook

TH

KY 192   *Rockcastle River*

Now let's get hiking. After crossing Sublimity Bridge and turning left, walk about 5 minutes on the road until you see the trailhead on your right for the Bee Rock Loop Trail #529, marked with white diamonds. The trail begins with a steady climb to the Bee Rock Overlook, which commands a splendid view of the Rockcastle River. Follow the trail up the hillside about 0.5 miles, along a small creek graced with several seasonal waterfalls and interesting rock formations. The trail then crosses a small wooden bridge and continues to bear east for a short distance, before meeting the Rockcastle Narrows Trail #503.

Turn right (south) and stay on the ridge top Bee Rock Loop Trail. In about 0.4 miles, you will pass through a thicket of mountain laurel (beautiful in early summer) and an unmarked trail will appear on your left. This is the continuation of the Bee Rock Loop Trail, but continue walking straight (yes, still south) for another five minutes to take the short spur to the Bee Rock Overlook.

Bee Rock? There must be another story here….. Legend has it that huge colonies of wild bees were living in the eroded sandstone that forms the bluffs overlooking the Rockcastle River. Well, these feral bees were messing with the local farmer's hives, introducing disease to the European strains, and adversely impacting pollination efforts and honey yields. Around the turn of the last century, a couple of young fellows threw a few sticks of dynamite into the crevices atop the bluff and folklore has it that honey came aburstin' outta' that rock and flowed all the way to the river. You can't make this stuff up.

From the Bee Rock Overlook, retrace your steps north about 0.5 miles, back to where the Rockcastle Narrows Trail #503 intersected the #529 trail, taking care NOT to turn right on the unmarked Bee Rock Loop Trail close to the overlook. After backtracking your steps, continue straight on #503. Look for a small, downed tree with a red paint patch, partially blocking the trail. (This tree has been here for years and let's hope it's still there when you try to navigate with these directions.) The Rockcastle Narrows Trail is not well marked at this point, but take a close look at the map and you should be fine. Trail #529 is blazed with red diamonds that with all the UV light exposure, the blazes look more dark orange.

After a few minutes of hiking you will come to a paved road that leads to a private farm. Cross the road to stay on the Rockcastle Narrows Trail. The path soon descends along a rock wall, with a nice rockhouse and an intermittent wet-weather waterfall. After traversing a wooded area, the trail takes a long, but gentle, descent down to the Rockcastle River.

Continue along the Rockcastle Narrows Trail until you near the river. If time and energy permits, turn left (north) on the Beach Narrows Trail to Beech Creek (yes, the spelling is accurate!) Take some time to walk and explore upstream along Beech Creek. This spur will add about 1.6 miles, round-trip, to your day.

If you hike the spur, trace your steps back along the Beach Narrows Trail. Just before rejoining the Rockcastle Narrows Trail there is a great lunch/snack spot on several huge boulders overlooking the river. This section of the Rockcastle is known as "The Narrows" due to a narrowing of the riverbed as a result of the large rocks that also form a small, but significant, series of rapids. "The Narrows" has flipped many a flat-water canoeist and provided lots of excitement for whitewater boaters.

The return hike along the Rockcastle Narrows Trail follows the river downstream for about 2.5 more miles. Along the way, be sure to notice the towering sandstone bluffs on your right. Once back to the campground, continue walking along the paved road until you reach the Sublimity Bridge.

Trail Map: http://goo.gl/THNrms

Side Trip:
Next time bring your camping gear and fishing rod. Both bait and fly fishermen have good luck here. Cane Creek is stocked with rainbow trout. You can also hike the Rockcastle Narrows East Trail on the other side of the river or the trail to Vanhook Falls (described elsewhere in this book.)

US Forest Service - London District
761 S. Laurel Road
London, KY 40744
Phone: (606) 864-4163
Web: http://goo.gl/ira2yP

4 Berea College Forest
aka Indian Fort Mountain Trail or The Pinnacles

A challenging set of trails running through Kentucky hardwood forests, leading to spectacular overlooks and sacred Indian grounds.

Trail Length: 2.2 to 7.2 miles

Facilities: No bathrooms or water available unless other events are scheduled.

Hours: Daily, sunrise to sunset.

Additional Information: Pets should be on leash. Hiking is free, but there may be a small entrance fee if an event is going on such as an art fair or performance.

Directions: From Lexington, head south on I-75. Take exit #76, traveling 1.5 miles east on KY 21, to downtown Berea. At the four-way stop (adjacent to Boone Tavern), continue on KY 21 another 3 miles, toward the town of Big Hill. Indian Fort Theatre will be on your left. There is NOT a sign posted here. (Do not confuse this with Berea Arena Theater, which you will also pass on your left.) If you miss the first entrance to the large parking lot, no worries, take the second one. Park at the top of the hill near the split rail fence, as the trailhead begins here.

Owned and managed by Berea College, Indian Fort Mountain includes an outdoor stage and is the site of the spring and fall Berea craft festivals. That said, when other activities are scheduled, admission may be required and crowds can be quite dense. Thankfully, despite periods of heavy use, trails remain mostly void of hiker debris. During the week you may even have the place to yourself.

After parking, enter through the split rail opening and follow the paved path to the stage area. From there you will see the trail and a large sign announcing: *Indian Fort Mountain Sacred Place of Prehistoric Man Hopewell Culture Period 100 BC – 400 AD.* A sign like that certainly makes one want to tread lightly. Widely acclaimed as a sacred mountain ceremonial site, discovered artifacts have been attributed to the Hopewell Amerindian culture. Previous research has identified 17 walls built by earlier Indian communities, essentially creating a fortress atop the mountain. Since 1875 the college has held Mountain Day on this site.

The trail begins with a steep ascent on a wide dirt path. If this makes you the least bit tired or discouraged, stay with it——you'll soon be rewarded with spectacular views and well-maintained trails. Shortly after your climb, you will come to a Y in the trail. The left branch will take you to the West Pinnacle and the right branch to the East Pinnacle. You can take a spur to either pinnacle, then return to this junction and on back to the parking lot. Alternately, you can view this junction as the beginning of a large adventure loop with spurs to each of the pinnacles.

A left at this Y will take you along a very nice trail to the West Pinnacle and views of Berea and northern Madison County. Two lower trails, Devil's Hollow and Walnut, partially encircle the pinnacle, before abruptly ending on the north side. Although lesser used, these trails are a wildflower wonderland during the spring, including larkspur and buttercup.

Instead of returning back to the Y junction, hike east on the rocky saddle. The trail becomes a roller coaster running from west to east. The saddle soon climbs to a well-maintained ridge-top trail with views to the north and the south. The next saddle is more of a smooth English riding saddle, before scrambling up again on the spine of the next rocky ridge. You'll be pleasantly amazed at the well-placed foot- and handholds, adorned with the occasional wild geranium and columbine. The next ridge top takes you to Indian Fort Lookout and Devil's Kitchen.

You'll quickly discover that the trails are not well marked up here, if marked at all. If a little more solitude is desired, be sure to take the spur to Eagles Nest (0.6 miles one-way) or Buzzards Roost (0.8 miles one-way). From the latter trail, you can go all the way to Robe and Basin Mountains. The views up here are spectacular with Pilot Knob and the Cumberland Escarpment just to the east. The Cumberland Escarpment (also known as the Pottsville Escarpment) forms the western boundary of the Cumberland Plateau. From any of these lookouts, it's fun to watch the soaring vultures ride the thermals rising from the valleys below.

On your way back down the trail, another spur takes you to the East Pinnacle and more views of the knobs of eastern Kentucky. Wild berries (black and blue) abound here. After visiting the East Pinnacle, return to the Y junction, then it's all downhill to the parking lot. By now you're probably out of water and beginning to think about dinner.

Trail Map: https://goo.gl/ZEPMyN

Side Trips:
Did someone say dinner? Try the casual Main Street Café or Boone Tavern (if you brought a change of clothes). Berea is also a great place for finding that special gift, if you're so inclined. The Kentucky Artisan Center at exit #77 showcases many of the arts and handicrafts of the region.

Berea College Forest at Indian Fort Theatre
Big Hill Road (KY 21)
Berea, KY 40403
Web: https://goo.gl/ycTp4r

5 Bernheim Arboretum and Research Forest

A lot of German perseverance and a drop or two of whiskey has protected 14,000 acres of Kentucky heartland.

Trail Length: As much or as little as you want to go in a day.

Facilities: Visitor Center, gift shop, café, water, bathrooms, and several paved trails with limited-ability access.

Hours: Basically 9 am-5 pm, and up to 9 pm, depending on the season. See their web site for specific hours.

Fees: Bernheim is free Monday through Friday; but an "Environmental Impact Fee" is charged Saturday, Sunday, and holidays: $5 per passenger car, minivan or motorcycle; $10 for passenger vans and RVs.

Additional Information: Pets on leash are permitted on trails. Please remember to clean up after them.

Directions: From Lexington, drive west on US 60 (Versailles Road). Take the Bluegrass Parkway for 46 miles. Get off at the Springfield/Bardstown exit #25. Follow KY 245/US 150 for 18 miles. The entrance to Bernheim is on your left.

Isaac W. Bernheim (1848-1945), a young German immigrant, arrived in the United States in 1867 with $4 to his name. That's less than $65 in today's dollars or enough to pay your monthly cell phone bill. He toiled as a peddler, riding horseback through the hills of Pennsylvania, until his horse died and he was forced to find a new livelihood. Bernheim then moved to Kentucky, gained a foothold in the whiskey distilling business, and established the I.W. Harper premium brand of bourbon whiskey.

In 1928, Bernheim bought 14,000 acres south of Louisville and northwest of Bardstown for $1 per acre, as the land had been stripped for mining iron ore. He then hired Frederick Law Olmsted (the "father" of landscape architecture and creator of several other renowned American urban gardens such as Central Park in New York) to work his magic. Bernheim Forest was then given in trust to the people of Kentucky for nature, art, and educational activities and opened in 1950. You may want to lift your glass to Isaac in a nod of thanks.

Opportunities at Bernheim are endless, with 35 miles of hiking and biking trails, gardens to stroll in, and water features to contemplate. If you have kids or less active adults along, you may want to check out the Visitor Center (the first certified Platinum LEED building in a multi-state area); the Canopy Tree Walk; the

Fire Tower Loop (occasionally open for climbing to the top); or the I Spy Trail (get directions and a list of items inside the Center).

There are also many short hikes, including the Lake Nevin Loop (1.3 miles); the Rock Run Loop (0.5 miles and excellent for wildflowers in the spring); or the Sun and Shade Loop (0.75 miles). Trail descriptions and maps can be found on the web site listed below.

For more ambitious hikers, you basically have two options. The Elm Lick Trail is a 5.0-mile hike that starts ridge top, before dropping down to parallel Elm Lick Creek. Of course you'll have to climb back up to the ridge again. The 13.75-mile Millennium Trail is not for the faint of heart. If you plan on hiking the Millennium, you must sign in at the Visitor Center or the trailhead. The trail is closed if a Heat Advisory is in effect. Despite traversing several creeks, most of the water here is seasonal and hikers should be fully prepared with water of their own.

Bernheim is also home to a small lake and several ponds; paved multi-use trails; interesting garden sculptures; and picnic areas. Guided tours, classes, and special programs are frequently offered throughout the year. See their web site for a full calendar of events.

Trail Maps: bernheim.org/general-info/trails/

Side Trip:
With Bardstown only 15 minutes away, there are a ton of touristy and historical things to do. Of course, distillery tours are another option. But for a more reverent experience, take time to experience the Abbey of Gethsemani, the 150-year old home for Roman-Catholic Trappist monks located about 40 minutes south of

Bernheim. Their singing is intensely beautiful. The monastery is known for their handmade bourbon fruitcake, bourbon fudge, and cheese. Hiking trails are also available. The address is 3642 Monks Road, Hwy 247, Trappist, KY 40051. See www.monks.org for more information.

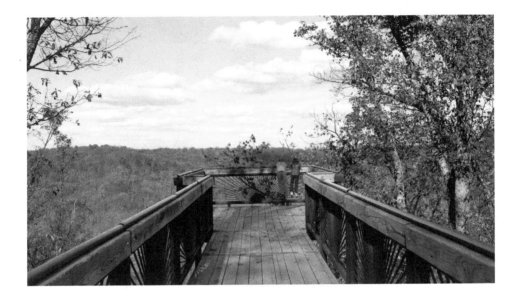

Bernheim Arboretum and Research Forest
2499 Clermont Road
Clermont, KY 40110
Phone: (502) 955-8512
Web: bernheim.org

6 Blue Licks State Park Nature Preserve

Walk along a portion of the original Buffalo Trace in this history-filled park, home to the extremely rare Short's Goldenrod.

Trail Length: 0.4 to 5 miles

Facilities: Restrooms, picnic tables and shelters, campground, lodge, cabins, pool, playground, and museum.

Hours: Daily, sunrise to sunset.

Additional Information: The Pioneer Museum has limited hours during the off-season. Check the website for posted hours; you can also call to schedule an appointment. Pets on leash are allowed in the park, but not in the nature preserve.

Directions: Traveling east from where North Broadway crosses under I-75, Broadway becomes Paris Pike. Drive approximately 13.3 miles and you'll find yourself at the Paris by-pass. Turn left on US 27 N / US 68 E. In a few miles, US 27 N will veer off to the left; stay on US 68 E. The bypass will end in 4.3 miles; turn left on US 68 E. Drive 11.3 miles; turn left on US 68 E at the flashing yellow light. Go another 9.8 miles. Just prior to the stone bridge overpass, turn left into Blue Licks Battlefield State Resort Park.

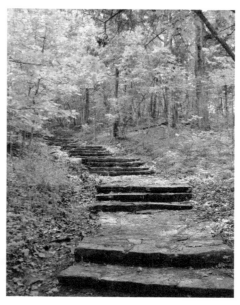

Widely acclaimed as the site of the "last battle of the revolution," the park honors those men of the Kentucky militia who bravely fought and died here in 1782. Despite Cornwallis' surrender at Yorktown, countless smaller battles continued to break out between those loyal to the crown and those fighting for American independence. Aided by almost 300 Indians, 50 Loyalists ambushed 182 members of Kentucky's militia on this hilltop overlooking the Licking River. Led in battle by Colonel John Todd (one of Lexington's founding fathers), Stephen Trigg, and Daniel Boone, this 15-minute battle left nearly 80 Kentuckians dead, almost 7% of

Indian Run

US 68

Monument

Pioneer
Museum

TH

Buffalo Trace
Trail

Blue Licks
Park Entrance

Licking
River Trail

Heritage
Trail

US 68

Tanner
Station

Licking River

Kentucky County's male population at the time. Dedicated in 1928, a large monument was erected and a pioneer museum built to keep that history alive.

The stonework of the museum itself is a work of art. Built from local limestone gathered from the Licking River and topped with a slate roof, the building was expanded in 1935 to house the many artifacts found within the park. Excavations from the old salt lick produced Mastodon tusks and jawbones, and skulls from hairy musk ox and bison, some of which are on display in the museum. Bone flutes, awls, and needles, as well as stone pipes and tools, provide evidence of the Indian communities who once thrived here. Another room houses artifacts from pioneer life, including looms, woodworking tools, and a three-quarter rope bed. The museum is perfect for kids——full of cool stuff but small enough for those with short attention spans.

The discovery of Short's Goldenrod (named after Louisville physician and amateur botanist Charles Short), led to additional land purchases to protect this endangered plant, which previously was believed to exist only in southern Indiana. Subsequently the original park boundaries were expanded an additional 53 acres and as a result the Preserve is actually located within the park's borders. The goldenrod blooms in late August until the first frost and can be seen in several locations throughout the Preserve. Another rare and threatened plant, the Great Plains ladies'-tresses orchid, can also be found blooming here in late September to early October.

The hiking here is not great, but the rich mixture of history and nature allows you to hike 5 miles and not even think about the distance. The Buffalo Trace Trail is short, only two-tenths of a mile, but connects you to the longer Heritage Trail, which follows along the Licking River. A note of warning——much of the Heritage Trail has full sun exposure and can get quite hot in the summer. This trail leads you past a replica of an old "fort" where Tanner Station, a salt-making operation, was once located. The kids will love climbing the ladder to the second floor loft. Further along the trail you pass the site of the original Blue Lick Springs and the former site of the plush Arlington Hotel, a 300-room resort built in the early 1800s. All that remains today are a soggy marsh populated with native cane and the memory of maids in white pinafores.

The Licking River Trail is a combination of hardwood forest and some open road along the river. But this is a good place to spot pileated woodpeckers, great blue herons, yellow finches, and blue birds. The Indian Run Trail is completely wooded and a good choice for spring wildflower viewing.

Side Trip:

To complete your visit you may want to throw in a tent and sleeping bag, and make a night of it. The park offers a host of amenities including canoe trips, live music, interpretive walks, and buffet dining. See their website for a complete list of activities and special events.

Blue Licks State Resort Park
Highway 68
Mt. Olivet, KY 41064-0066
Phone: (859) 289-5507
Toll Free: (800) 443-7008
**Web: parks.ky.gov/findparks/
resortparks/bl**

7 Boone Station State Historic Site

A short walk through time, perfect for young children and Kentucky history buffs.

Trail Length: 1 mile or less

Facilities: Port-a-potty; no water.

Hours: April 1–October 31, 9 am–5 pm (posted sign says closes at dusk.)

Directions: Out of Lexington, drive east on Richmond Road. From the intersection with Man O' War Boulevard, travel 5.8 miles to the small hamlet of Athens. (Be sure to pronounce Athens with a long-A vowel sound; otherwise you'll end up in the capital of Greece.) Turn left at the four-way stop sign, on North Cleveland (KY 1973). Drive 0.2 miles, then turn right on Gentry Road. You'll see a sign to Boone Station, which is another 0.4 miles on your left. If the black farm gate is closed, park on the gravel and enter through the small fence opening on your right.

Originally part of an American Revolutionary War land grant, Daniel Boone and his family moved here from Fort Boonesborough in 1779. Boone and his cohorts built a stockade for protection and 15-20 families eventually moved in. Cultural resource analysts, in cooperation with the University of Kentucky, have used conductivity and magnetometry surveys to find remnants of several original stone foundations built on the site.

Upon his death in 1991, Robert Channing "Chan" Strader, a descendent of Boone's, deeded the park over to the state of Kentucky. His will mandated that the property always remain a park and that the "State Park Commission not do any major altering of the lay of the land, and build very few buildings upon it." The state has complied.

The 46-acre park consists of mostly open fields and replicas of a small stockade and several lean-tos. At the top of the gravel road, on the back side of the black

barn, you will find an old faded map of the area. The park is touted as offering a one-mile self-guided trail, which can only be loosely translated as "meander through the fields at your own pace." A mowed path bisects the park and in some places continues along the perimeter of the rolling property.

An adjacent field holds a large stone monument to several Boone relatives who purportedly have been buried at the Station, including two of Daniel's brothers and one of his sons, Israel (who was killed at the Battle of Blue Licks).

Side Trip:
Before heading out to the park, stop at your favorite fabric store and pick up a half-yard (or more) of furry material. Using your best sewing or stapling skills, fashion a coonskin hat for every child in your party. Pack some hardtack and spring water, and you're ready for a picnic.

Boone Station State Historic Site
240 Gentry Road
Athens, KY 40509
**Web: http://www.parks.ky.gov/parks/
historicsites/boone-station/**

8 Buckley Wildlife Sanctuary

Step back in time by crossing the large, limestone threshold of the Emma Buckley Nature Center or quietly slip through the side door of the bird blind to watch the tufted titmouse dance on the edge of the feeder.

Trail Length: 0.3 to 2.9 miles

Facilities: Nature Center, picnic pavilion, bird blind, restrooms, drinking water.

Hours: Trails are open to the public Wednesday through Friday, 8 am-5 pm; Saturday and Sunday 8 am-6 pm. The Nature Center is open by appointment. Closed holidays.

Additional Information: A small $4 donation for adults and $3 for children (16 and under) is requested (about the same as a fancy latte, except no change is given.) The best time to visit is in the morning or late afternoon if contemplative bird watching is your thing.

Directions: Head west on Versailles Road (US 60). Bear right in Versailles (towards Frankfort), and drive another 7 miles. Turn left on Grassy Spring Road (County Road 3360 S). Follow the signs to the sanctuary by turning right on CR 1659 N; left on CR 1964 (at the Millville Fire House and Community Center); and right on Germany Road. The park is 1.5 miles on the left.

Emma must have sure loved Clyde when she dedicated most of this land as a memorial to her late husband. Managed by the Central Kentucky Audubon Society and the Life Adventure Center, the sanctuary covers 374 square acres situated above the Kentucky River.

After parking, if staff is not available, drop your fee in the wishing well (on the honor system, of course). Then stroll over to the large sign and find the guest register, brochures, and notebooks for the self-guided trails.

As for hiking, the red trail covers 1.4 miles of meadow and lightly wooded areas, with the yellow trail appendage adding another 0.6 miles of larger, more mature trees. The white bunny trail, covering an astounding 0.3 miles, is perfect for the toddler just breaking in those new Vibram soles. The one-mile blue trail circles the pond before crossing the road and heading back up to the Nature Center.

The Nature Center is filled with a fascinating collection of animal skulls, painted egg replicas, a live beehive, and various entomological collections (bugs bugs and more bugs) from the 1960s. Given the slow pace of natural evolution and an occasional light dusting, these specimens look brand new.

Peering through the one-way windows of the Marion Lindsey Bird Blind, you might catch a glimpse of a ruby-throated hummingbird or a red-bellied woodpecker. Don a tweed cap or hang your opera glasses about your neck, and during the winter months you'll be sure to sight at least a slate-colored junco or two. A morning visit when the kids are in school promises even more avian variety.

Buckley is the ideal outing for kids needing to run, canter, and banter about nature. The Sanctuary is open to school groups and environmental education activities. A large covered pavilion, complete with bathrooms, needs only a picnic basket for a lovely outing. Special events may include wildflower searches, stargazing, geocaching, various talks including bats of the Bluegrass and exotic reptiles, and the annual Audubon Christmas bird count.

Side Trips:
On the way home, stop by Paul Sawyer Galleries (3445D Versailles Road) or Rebecca-Ruth Candies (3295 Versailles Road) for yet another taste of central Kentucky. If something stronger is needed for your palate, stop by for a tour of the Woodford Reserve Distillery (7855 McCracken Pike).

Buckley Wildlife Sanctuary
1305 Germany Road
Frankfort, KY 40601
Phone: (859) 873-5711
Web: http://goo.gl/ARWFsd

9 Camp Nelson Civil War Heritage Park

Hiking trails, historic relics, and an eye-opening look at how colored troops and their families were treated during the Civil War.

Trail Length: 0.5 to 4 miles

Facilities: Interpretive Center, historical home tour, bathrooms, and drinking water.

Hours: Trails are open dawn to dusk. The Park is open Tuesday through Saturday 9 am-5 pm. Guided tours of the house are available Tuesday through Saturday, 10 am-4 pm.

Additional Information: No entrance fees and all of the tours are free. Most of the grounds are exposed to the elements. That breeze may feel heavenly in the summer and biting during the winter. Some of the interpretive signs along the trails are difficult to read due to sun exposure. Pets on leash are good.

Directions: From the intersection of Nicholasville Road and Man O' War, continue heading south on US 27. Travel 14 miles, taking the bypass around the town of Nicholasville. Turn left at the brown park sign. Don't worry if you miss this one – 0.8 miles later you can take the next left and double back to the Camp on the service road. Park in the small lot, between the "White House" and the Interpretive Center.

The park brings on an eerie wave of peace and deep reverence for those soldiers and their families who endured the Civil War. Camp Nelson highlights the unique role Kentucky played during the war, particularly with regard to the colored

troops (the vernacular used at the time and still used by historians today).

During the War, Camp Nelson operated as a small city, serving 80,000 Union soldiers, including 10,000 African–Americans. The park itself is comprised of 525 of the original 4,000 acres that served as a Union Army Supply Depot, Enlistment, and Training

Post. Preserved on the grounds are six earthen and two stone forts overlooking Hickman Creek.

If possible, begin at the Interpretive Center. The docents are a wealth of knowledge for the most arduous of history buffs, yet can reel yarns to entertain the youngest of children. Inside you'll find period artifacts and constructed models of what life was like inside an army encampment during the 1860s. Full-size replicas of a covered wagon, hospital ward, artillery display, and refugee camp will leave you wondering how they survived the War without anesthesia or potable water. Be sure to pick up a trail map as you leave the building.

The Union Army appropriated the "White House," originally built and owned by the Perry family, for use as the commissary and as the Quartermaster's office quarters. The house showcases period furnishings from the 1860s and reminders of its use during military occupation. If you want to tour the house during the week, it's a good idea to call ahead and confirm someone is available to guide tours. Guided tours are also available for the interpretive trails.

Five interpretive trails, comprising almost 5 miles, crisscross the grounds. With the exception of the wooded Fort Jones/Overlook Trail, all of the trails are essentially mowed paths through open fields. Be sure to note on the map that you must walk both the Fort Putnam Loop Trail and the Long Fort Trail to access the Fort Jones Trail. (Despite the notation of a parking lot at the far eastern edge of the park, this lot is no longer open to the public.)

The Emancipation Proclamation, signed by President Lincoln in 1863, only freed slaves in the rebellious states (those that had seceded from the Union).

Consequently, many other slaves enlisted in the Union army to secure their freedom. Many of the colored troops at Camp Nelson also brought their families. A refugee camp sprung up to house over 3,000 women and children. Sadly, in November of 1864 (four months before the War came to an end), 400 woman and children were ejected from Camp Nelson. Sadly, that winter, 102 of them died from exposure and disease.

Before you leave Camp Nelson Civil War Heritage Park, stand near the old tobacco barn in the middle of the field. From this location you can see both the old bourbon warehouses near the Kentucky River and the mass grave where the remains of hundreds of colored women and children still lie. The intermittent crowing of over 200 roosters rising from the farm along Hickman Creek reminds us that we're still in Kentucky.

Trail Map: http://goo.gl/1KbyVT

Side Trip:
After the war ended and Camp Nelson closed, Reverend John Fee (abolitionist and founder of Berea College) bought 130 acres of land, including part of the refugee camp, and established the Ariel Academy to provide educational and spiritual training to the remaining colored families. Remnants of this camp can be seen in the small hamlet of Hall, KY where the Fee Memorial Chapel is still standing. The community of Hall is located off Hall Road, just south of the park and west of US 27.

Camp Nelson Civil War Heritage Park
6614 Danville Road
Nicholasville, KY 40356
Phone: (859) 881-5716 or (859) 492-3115
Web: www.campnelson.org

10 Camp Wildcat Civil War Battlefield

Site of the first battle of the Civil War fought on Kentucky soil.

Trail Length: 2.5 miles

Facilities: Interpretive signs; vault toilets.

Hours: Trails are open dawn to dusk.

Additional Information: No entrance fees. Pets must be restrained or on leash at all time.

Directions: Heading south on I-75, take exit #49. Turn left (east) on KY 909. Drive 0.6 miles. Turn right (south) on US 25. Go another 0.7 miles. Turn left on Hazel Patch Road. Right after the railroad tracks, bear left on Wildcat Happy Hollow Road. Follow the gravel road for 2.5 miles. Park in the large lot on your right, near the interpretive signs.

Civil War buffs and hikers alike have lots of opportunities here. The trails are relatively short and easy, but direct access to the Sheltowee Trace Trail creates lots of other choices for getting outside.

The 1.0-mile main trail to the battlefield site leaves from the parking area, just between the bathrooms and the shelter housing many of the interpretive signs. The trail leads up Wildcat Mountain where, on October 21, 1861, Union and Confederate forces first exchanged musket fire in Kentucky. The trail is wide and lightly-graveled, with benches and more interpretive signs sprinkled along the way. A half-mile into your walk, on your left, there is a small hobbit cave if you happened to bring Bilbo or any of his cousins along.

From here, the trail continues through deciduous woods before ascending to Hoosier Knob, a natural fortification with cliffs on three sides, easily defended from approaching Confederate troops. There is a small cannon atop the knob, with 360-degree views of the countryside (particularly after the leaves have fallen). Be sure to read about the earthen berms and trenches built atop the knob. Although the battle was a decisive Union victory, the blue coats lost 4 men in battle and more than 200 to disease once the battle ended. Similar numbers held for the Confederates.

After hiking back to the trailhead, there are a few other sites to visit. Just across from the entrance to the parking lot, on the other side of the gravel road, you will see a short flight of wooden stairs leading to the Infantry Ridge Trail. At the top of the steps, the trail makes a T. Turning left (south) will take you to Hospital Rock, a small rockhouse, where injured Union soldiers were treated. There are a number of interpretive signs along the way.

Alternately, turning right (north) at the T will take you to several monuments commemorating the battle. Following the gravel road a bit further, a spur trail leads down to Robinson Spring. There's not much water flowing, but sometimes every drop helps.

All of these hiking distances are short. But if you're interested in more mileage, a section of the Sheltowee Trace Trail #100 passes through here. It's 8 miles one-way to the Rockcastle River, but all of the gravel roads are easily walkable.

Side Trip:
Reenactments are held the third weekend in October. For more information see http://wildcatreenactment.com/

You are also very close to the Rockcastle River Trading Company, located just a smidge further north on US 25. In addition to garden-related shopping opportunities, they have recently added a Proven Winners® Botanical Trail. See their web site for hours and special events http://joncarloftis.com/rrtc/ or call (606) 843-0854. They are also on FB.

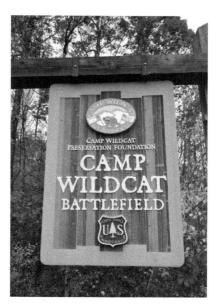

Camp Wildcat Preservation Foundation
PO Box 1510
London, KY 40743
Tel: (606) 864-9776
Web: wildcatbattlefield.org

USDA Forest Service
London Ranger District
761 South Laurel Drive
London, KY 40744
Tel: (606) 864-4163
Web: fs.usda.gov/dbnf/

11 Capitol View Park

This urban park has something for everyone, from hiking and mountain biking to ball games, all accented with views of the state capitol and the Kentucky River.

Trail Length: 0.4 to 8 miles

Facilities: Bathrooms and drinking water are available on a seasonal basis; picnic shelters, grills.

Hours: Summer hours (April-October), 8 am-11 pm (except during softball tournaments); winter hours (November-March), the park closes at dark.

Additional Information: Some trails can be quite muddy after a heavy rain. Weekends and weeknights can get crowded during various ball seasons.

Directions: From the intersection of Versailles Road (US 60) and New Circle Road, continue heading west out of Lexington. Travel approximately 19.6 miles on US 60, toward Frankfort (taking the Versailles Bypass and crossing over I-64). Turn left on KY 676/421, also known as the East-West Connector. Drive another 1.6 miles. Turn right on Glenn's Creek Road and then a quick left at the sign for the park.

Comprised of 150 acres located across the river from the Kentucky State Capitol, this park is truly a multi-sport complex. Think of a semi-circle dart board, with the core providing ample parking; the inner ring featuring sports fields and basketball courts; and the outer ring containing most of the hiking and mountain biking trails. The park is largely confined by the banks of the Kentucky River and bisected by the East-West Connector (KY 676).

After entering the park from Glenn's Creek Road, the first right will take you to a parking lot and kiosk with a posted map of the area and the following playful disclaimer: *This map is not drawn to scale nor does it meet any particular standards for accuracy or precision.* Further, do not rely on the mailbox located at the kiosk to contain maps.

However, your chances of getting lost at Fayette Mall are much better than at Capitol View Park.

Exploring the trails at a hikers pace allows time to enjoy some of the mature hardwoods in the area. Large-girthed sycamore, wild cherry, hickory, and oak can be found near the river's bank. An abundance of deer flaunt their white-tailed flags in an urban park setting within sight of where hunting laws are written and passed.

The network of trails has been expanded and fine-tuned by various mountain bike enthusiasts. The terrain is primarily level hardpack dirt, although the trails adjacent to the river itself can be steep and muddy in places. Most of the trails are single track (wide enough for only one cyclist or hiker at a time), and include some tight, twisty sections. However, the non-technical nature of most of the trail system makes it a good place for youngsters just learning to ride and others wanting an easier day in the bike saddle. Theoretically, hikers have the right-of-way on the trails and bikers should give way to those on foot.

The park has two picnic shelters (no electricity), grills, and river access for fishing and swimming. Be cautious, though, as the access point is at a bend in the Kentucky River and prone to fast moving current most times of the year. The posted sign says it well: *Swim at your own risk.*

Trail Map: http://goo.gl/ecauXe

Side Trip:
Every Kentuckian, by birth or by driver's license, needs to see the Beaux-Arts style Kentucky State Capitol building (702 Capitol Avenue), which includes many French-inspired interior elements. This 1904 structure replaced an earlier capitol building, shortly after William Goebel was assassinated just prior to his inauguration as governor. We suppose it was easier to build anew rather than get the bloodstains out. The Capitol is open for tours during the week, guided or not, and is quite beautiful, particularly when most of the legislators are gone.

Capitol View Park
Corner of State Hwy 676 and Glenn's Creek Road
Frankfort, KY 40601
Web: http://goo.gl/orgjcG

12 Carter Caves State Park

No spelunking necessary——the park features several natural rock bridges, so there are plenty of hiking opportunities above ground.

Trail Length: 4.5 miles, with several options for more or less.

Facilities: Welcome Center, lodge, campground, cabin rentals, golf course, swimming pool, cave tours, and picnic areas and shelters.

Hours: Be off the trails by dark.

Additional Information: Pets are permitted on leash.

Directions: Follow I-64 east past Morehead. Take exit #161 at Olive Hill. Turn left (north) on US 60 E. Drive 1.4 miles. Take another left on KY 182. Drive 2.7 miles. Cross the bridge over Tygarts Creek, and then take an immediate left into the park. Drive a short distance. Turn right into the Welcome Center. Park here or in the overflow parking lot across the road.

While most people think of Carter Caves State Park and Resort for its below ground activities, that same karst topography that formed the caves has been working above ground to create natural bridges, towering cliffs, and impressive rock houses and faces.

There are several short to medium-length trails in the park, providing easy access to most of the highlights Carter Caves has to offer. The best map can be picked up for free inside the Welcome Center—it has lots of nice topo lines and trail descriptions. You can also download a good map off their web page, using the link found below.

The Three Bridges Trail is an easy 3.5-mile hike showcasing three of the natural rock bridges found in the park. Interestingly, because there are so many other access points to this trail, many visitors simply take the shortcut routes to each bridge and few actually hike the entire trail. So defy national data touting laziness in Kentucky and actually hike the whole thing!

Beginning at the Welcome Center, the red-blazed Three Bridges Trail begins right across the road, near an abandoned saltpeter mine. Turn left on the trail to hike it clockwise. After crossing two wooden bridges, at mile 0.45 you will come to a set of wooden stairs leading to a natural area designated for rappelling and climbing. This makes a nice diversion, particularly if athletes are in the area, demonstrating their admirable skills.

Shortly after the wooden stairs, bear left on the trail to descend a steep set of steps, painstakingly built from stone, leading to Fern Bridge. While there is a small traditional footbridge flanked by ferns, look up to see the beautiful rock bridge arched high above you. Here the rock has cleaved in sections, allowing light to filter between the stone sections forming the bridge.

A third of a mile past Fern Bridge is a small detour to Raven Bridge. Turn right on Raven Bridge Trail and almost immediately you will see the slender, but less than spectacular, stone formation. Return to the Three Bridges Trail and continue on your way.

Approximately two miles from the trailhead, the path follows under some nice cliffs and rock overhangs. Unfortunately, this will be the signal that you are a 5-10 minute walk from the back of the Lewis Caveland Lodge. Ignore the sounds of the HVAC units and air vents to continue your quest for solitude.

At this point the trail surface becomes lightly graveled. Stay on the downhill until you see the sign for Smoky Bridge. Turn right to follow the trail under the bridge and then back up the drainage. Smoky is an impressive structure with a seasonal stream running beneath it. As a result of its easy access, the area around the rock bridge is well worn, but it's also easy to understand its popularity.

Continue on the Three Bridges Trail, crossing the paved road to the campground, until you get back to the Welcome Center. Refill your water bottles, take a bathroom break, and head out for the next adventure.

Two other trails leave from the Welcome Center. The Natural Bridge Trail leaves from the western side of the parking lot. It's a very easy 0.5-mile walk to yet another impressive rock bridge with a paved park road traveling atop and a wide, gurgling stream running beneath. There are several picnic areas in the vicinity, so again expect to see lots of people.

The 1.5-mile Horn Hollow Trail leaves from the eastern side of the Welcome Center parking lot. This loop trail is a bit hilly and takes you past the opening to Horn Hollow Cave, which is rather interesting. Cave Branch flows from a large rockhouse close to the road, but is also rather scenic. This is probably the best trail for wildflower viewing in the springtime.

A really great hike is the 0.8-mile Box Canyon Trail. It's about a five-minute drive from the Welcome Center and is located in the Cascade Caverns Nature Preserve on the south side of the park. To reach the trailhead, exit the park and turn south on KY 182. Drive for 1.6 miles. Turn right on KY 209. Drive another 0.7 miles. Turn left into the Cascade Caves parking lot where many tours begin.

The Box Canyon trail leaves from the far end of the parking lot and forms a loop, passing under some beautiful rock walls and rockhouses. Cascade Bridge, a natural stone arch, is located at the far end of the loop. Chances are you will have this trail to yourself. This hike is also great for kids.

A major caveat of hiking Carter Caves is the sheer number of people who visit here, particularly in the summer. Although the trails are heavily shaded and cool air blows from the multitude of rock openings and spring-fed creeks, you are guaranteed to run into people and hear road noise along several sections of the trails. The major exception is the Box Canyon Trail.

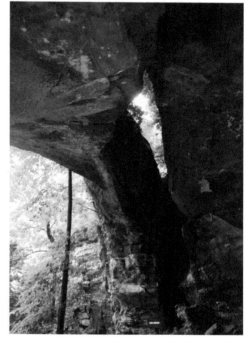

However, the shoulder seasons and even winter months hold promise of solitude and a quiet day on the trail. The spring flowers here can be gorgeous and the rock formations are even more impressive before the trees have leafed out, or in the fall when glorious autumnal colors abound.

Trail Map: http://goo.gl/ArhXCn

Side Trip:
Obviously you can take your hiking underground and sign up for any of the cave tours offered. Given its deceptive name, only hike to the Shangri La Arch, off the Carter Caves Cross Country Trail, if you really want to be thorough when you visit the park.

Carter Caves State Resort Park
344 Caveland Drive
Olive Hill, KY 41164
Phone: (606) 286-4411 or (800) 325-0059
Web: http://goo.gl/PZsTxM

Cave Run Lake

Located in the Eastern Highlands Region of eastern Kentucky, Cave Run Lake was formed in 1973 when the US Army Corps of Engineers dammed the Licking River as part of a larger flood control effort. Measuring 8270 acres, the lake is surrounded by the northern section of the Daniel Boone National Forest. Consequently, both the Corps and the US Forest Service have jurisdiction over the lake and surrounding woods.

There are 115 miles of trails surrounding Cave Run Lake, including a portion of the Sheltowee Trace (that runs the length of Daniel Boone National Forest). In addition to primitive camping, five campgrounds have been developed around the lake including three Recreational Areas (Clear Creek, Twin Knobs, and Zilpo); Clay Lick Boat-In; and White Sulphur Horse Camp.

The US Forest Service and the Kentucky Department of Fish and Wildlife Resources also manage the 7,610-acre Pioneer Weapons Management Area. The hunting grounds are marked with yellow signs and yellow-painted bands around some trees.

Unfortunately, the Tater Knob Fire Tower was destroyed by arson in December 2008. The Forest Service does not have plans to rebuild it at this time. You can still hike to the base of the tower, but there's not much left to see.

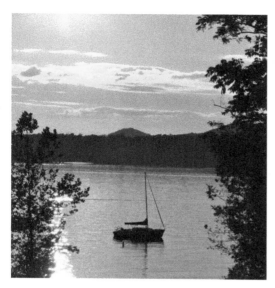

A Park Pass must be displayed at any of the six public boat ramps—Alfrey, Claylick, Poppin Rock, Long Bow, Scott Creek and Warix. A pass costs $3.00 for a one-day permit; $5.00 for a three-day permit; or $30.00 for an annual permit. Passes are available at the Forest Service office and from some local businesses.

None of the hiking trails require a permit. Detailed topo maps for the entire lake area can be obtained from outrageGIS mapping at outragegis.com.

Cave Run Lake
Cumberland Ranger District - Daniel Boone National Forest
2375 KY 801 South
Morehead, KY 40351
Phone: (606) 784-6428
Web: http://goo.gl/DT8Icx

13 Caney Trail Loop

Easy hiking with intermittent views of Cave Run Lake.

Trail Length: 8.5 miles

Facilities: Port-a-potty, picnic tables, grills.

Hours: None posted.

Additional Information: This is a multi-use trail open to hikers and equestrian riders. Please share the trail. No ATVs allowed.

Directions: Drive east on I-64. Take the Sharkey/Farmers exit #133. Turn right on KY 801 S. Continue driving south for 5.1 miles, through the 4-way stop intersection with US 60. Turn right on KY 826. You should see a sign for Stoney Cove Recreation Area. Drive another 0.8 miles, over the dam, and left into the recreation area. You'll probably want to park in the second lot on your left, just past the information kiosk. No parking pass is required.

Hike this trail in early spring for the wildflowers, during the dog days of summer for the swimming, and in the fall for the magnificent colors. The lake views are most prominent when the leaves are off the trees. But if the day is warm, pack a bathing suit and your lunch, and you're set for a day of woodland and waterland fun.

The Caney Trail, (#1226, marked with white diamonds) begins behind the information kiosk, a tenth of a mile up the gravel road. Near the top you'll see the trail intersect both left and right of the road. Most people hike the Caney Trail Loop clockwise, so take a left at this junction. Technically what you will be doing is hiking the Caney Trail on your way out and using the Sheltowee Trace Trail to complete the loop back to this same spot.

The forest is primarily deciduous hardwoods (the ones that drop their leaves in the fall)

and includes a lot of sons of birches and beeches. In a third of a mile you will see pine beetle damage and a new crop of sweet gum and maple quickly moving into the neighborhood. Views of Cave Run Lake will soon appear on your left.

In about two miles, the trail begins to follow the shoreline of Fishing Creek (a relatively large tributary of the lake). The trail remains wide and fairly flat with gentle undulations caused by seasonal creek crossings. About four miles from the trailhead is a nice cold-weather lunch spot, complete with logs to sit on and a fire pit for those hot dogs stashed in your pack.

The Caney Trail crosses under some power lines about 5.6 miles from the trailhead and joins the Sheltowee Trace Trail at mile marker 5.75. A left here would take you two miles to White Sulphur Horse Camp. Take a right on the Sheltowee Trace Trail, pass back under the power lines, and hike another 2.5 miles back to the Stoney Cove parking lot.

Side Trips:

After leaving Stoney Cove, turn right and go back over the dam. Turn left on KY 801, as if you were going back to the interstate. On your left you'll see the Minor E. Clark Fish Hatchery, one of the largest warm-water fish hatcheries in the US. Almost four million bass, muskellunge, walleye, and other fish are raised here before being released into Kentucky's waterways. Open year-round, dawn to dusk. Indoor tours are available 7 am–3 pm during the summer. Call 606-784-6872 for more information. Free.

If you're hungry, stop by Pig-Out Bar-B-Q, 110 KY Highway 801, just before the intersection with US 60. The pulled pork and homemade pies will leave you a pickin' and a grinnin'. And the wall ornaments are a taxidermists dream come true.

14 Furnace Arch Trail

An out-and-back trail leading to an exquisite arch named after a pig iron furnace.

Trail Length: 6 miles (round-trip)

Facilities: Pit toilets, picnic tables, and grills at trailhead. No water.

Hours: None posted.

Additional Information: This is a multi-use trail open to hikers and equestrian riders. Please share the trail.

Directions: Drive east on I-64. Take the Owingsville/Salt Lick exit #123. Turn right on US 60 E. Drive 6.6 miles. Turn right on KY 211 and take the dogleg through the town of Salt Lick. Drive another 3.7 miles and turn left on Clear Creek Road (KY 129). You should see a sign for the Zilpo Recreational Area. Go another 2.4 miles; turn right into the Clear Creek Picnic Area. Park in the small gravel lot.

After parking, the first thing you might notice is the Clear Creek Iron Furnace, which operated from 1839-75. In the mid-1850s, Kentucky was a major producer of pig iron used to make everything from railcar wheels to household items. At its peak, this furnace produced 3-4 tons of iron daily, and required 35 cords of wood to make the charcoal used to stoke the furnace. These furnaces were prevalent across eastern Kentucky until the forests were depleted and cheaper sources of iron ore were discovered in Alabama.

Clear Creek Lake

Clear Creek Furnace

TH

KY 127

Clear Creek Rd.

Glady Hollow Rd.
(dirt)

Furnace Arch

The unmarked trail to Furnace Arch begins at the end of the parking lot and across the small bridge that spans Clear Creek. A left turn on the far side of the bridge will take you south on the Sheltowee Trace Trail and to Furnace Arch. The trail ascends quickly up a series of switchbacks through hardwood forest. At 0.7 miles, you'll be at the top of a ridge near an old camp. The trial continues right, through bee balm, wild roses, and red bud trees. A half-mile of ridgetop hiking brings you to the next saddle, before gently climbing ridgetop again. If you're not intimately familiar with the thorny nature of smilax, you soon will be. At 2.25 miles, a trail comes in on your right. Don't get sidetracked, but continue straight up the trail to get to the arch.

Look sharp at mile 2.45 as the trail makes an abrupt right turn up and over a small rock outcropping. You should see hoof print marks on the rocks and a white diamond blaze and arrow pointing right. The sandy trail continues ridgetop to some large rocks, beautifully framed with mountain laurel.

After descending the s-turn in the trail, look up to your right to see Furnace Arch. Do not try and climb the fragile sandstone arch (strictly forbidden) but feel free to explore underneath. The contrast of green moss with the red sandstone makes a fetching combination. Large oaks and tulip poplars shade the base of the arch, while maples grow precariously from its cracks. This makes a great lunch spot and is perfect for contemplating why you don't get out more often.

From here you can continue hiking south on Sheltowee Trace Trail (for another 200 or so miles, if you like). Alternately, turn around and retrace your steps back to the trailhead and call it a day.

Side Trip:

After you leave the picnic area, be sure to stop at Clear Creek Market (on your left), where fish stories are limited to five minutes and 35 inches. This old-timey general store has a bit of everything including some outstanding homemade pies. Recent offerings included coconut, butterscotch, peanut butter, strawberry, blackberry, apple, and peach pies. Notices of jam cake and chocolate cheesecake were also posted. Life is good.

Web: sheltoweetrace.com

15 Central Kentucky Wildlife Refuge

Five hundred acres nestled within the arms of the North Rolling Fork and Carpenter Fork creeks, located at the foothills of Central Kentucky's knobs region.

Trail Length: 0.3 to 6.7 miles

Facilities: Plastic outhouse at parking lot; no drinking water available.

Hours: Daily, sunrise to sunset.

Additional Information: Pets are permitted on leash (how many wildlife refuges allow that?!) Despite the picnic tables you'll find, no picnicking is permitted.

Directions: From Lexington, follow Nicholasville Road south (US 27 S). About 23 miles from Man O' War Boulevard, hang a right on KY 34 W, toward Danville. Follow KY 34 all the way through town and out the other side. Once you hit the small burg of Parksville, take a left on County Road 1822. After 3 miles, CR 1822 Ts into KY 37. Turn right. Go 0.7 miles and take a left on Carpenter Creek Road. Currently there is not a street sign, but you will see a sign for the Refuge. The parking lot for CKWR will be another 0.7 miles on your left.

After parking in the small lot, you'll see the information kiosk at the start of the trail system. A large map is posted, and a very nice trail guide is available in the box. Grab your water bottle, take a considering glance at the port-a-potty (the only chance you'll have), and drop a few bucks into the donation box. Drop in more if you can. A non-profit organization, CKWR relies on our generosity.

The short gravel trail behind the kiosk will take you to the Mary Ashby Cheek Pavilion and Nature Center. CKWR uses this facility for school children, college students, and scout groups. (They even have grants available to defer transportation costs.) Here you will find the sign in/out notebook.

Established in the early 1960s, CKWR has worked diligently to preserve and enhance the flora and fauna of the area. Ponds have been built, trees planted, and meadows mowed to increase and protect the diversity of wildlife in the region.

This is one of those hiking and outdoor experiences with a trail for everyone. In general, the trails near the creeks and ponds are relatively short, flat, and wide, rendering them perfect for the younger set. Best of all, this place is quiet, although at the far end of Fork Trail you might find yourself singing "Oh, we'll kill that ol' red rooster when she comes…" and have visions of chicken and dumplings dancing in your head. Is it ever a bad time to commune with nature?

Be sure to point out the beaver activity near Island Pond to the kiddos and if they can walk to the intersection of Cross Trail and Brooks Hollow Trail, they'll love the small swinging bridge. Sturdy benches and viewing platforms are readily available. Make a mental note to yourself: Some of these trails are perfect for cross-country skiing.

Although it's not clear from the map, the Yellow Trail is a short half-mile loop off the Circle Trail, and the Waterfall Trail is a spur off of Yellow. But be forewarned. You must cross a small creek to view the modest waterfall, suggesting that the more spectacular the fall will be, the wetter your boots might become to get there.

As you move to the far end of the Refuge, the trails become much narrower and downright strenuous for short periods of time. If you're up for a short, but rigorous climb, be sure to hike up the Ridge Trail. Coming from either direction off Circle Trail, you begin with a sharp ascent up the spine of Huckleberry Ridge, which is steeper than the spires of Westminster Abbey. Thankfully, the climb gives way to a roller coaster of grassy spines and saddles through peaceful hardwoods, offering beautiful views in all directions.

If you want to see the Fred Loetscher Bird Blind, go back to the parking lot and follow the short trail between the road and the caretaker's house. Unfortunately, this is not the most ideal location for a bird blind. Fred would probably feel a little regret.

The Wildflower Trail is located somewhat off site. After leaving the parking lot, head back on Carpenter Creek Road. Right before you cross back over the bridge spanning North Rolling Fork, you will see a small parking area on your left and an old farm gate. Park here (or close by) and follow this short uneventful trail along the creek itself.

Side Trip:
Driving back through Danville, allow yourself to be enticed by the long-revered Burke's Bakery or the more eclectic Hub Coffee House and Café, both found on West Main.

Central Kentucky Wildlife Refuge
Carpenter Creek Road
Parksville, KY 40464
Web: ckwr.org

16 Civil War Fort at Boonesboro

A short walk, up a steep hill, to a large overlook of Kentucky history.

Trail Length: 1.4 miles total, out-and-back.

Facilities: Picnic tables, vault toilet.

Hours: October through April, 9 am-5 pm; May through September 9 am-8 pm.

Additional Information: You can bring Fido on this one. But as the sign says, with an overabundance of caution, *Be Cautious of Poison Ivy / Oak & Barbwire.* And to think, we were worried about rifle fire...

Directions: South of Lexington and north of Richmond, take exit #95 off I-75. Turn on KY 627, heading north towards Fort Boonesborough State Park. Shortly after passing the park, KY 627 crosses the Kentucky River. Turn right (southeast) on KY 1924 (aka Four Mile Road or Ford Road). In a little over a mile you will see a small parking area, mural, and signage for the Civil War Fort.

Most Kentuckians are familiar with Fort Boonesborough, founded in 1775 by Daniel and his cohorts. But did you know that almost 100 years later, the Union Army built a Civil War fort on the opposite side of the Kentucky River? Well, the Winchester-Clark County Tourism Commission and the Kentucky Department of Tourism have joined forces to add this piece of history to Kentucky's Civil War Heritage Trail.

As Union and Confederate soldiers worked their way back and forth across the state, the Kentucky River presented both opportunities and challenges. At the time, only two bridges spanned the river—one at Frankfort and the other at Camp Nelson, south of Nicholasville. In addition, over 50 fords and ferries carried people and goods across the waterway. To limit Confederate activity in the region and guard the ford and ferry at Boonesboro, a redoubt or enclosed earthen fort, surrounded by a ditch and abatis was built high above the Kentucky River. The fort was completed in 1863 and only occupied as needed, until 1865.

After parking in the small lot, the first thing you'll notice is the long mural, composed of 12 different panels, depicting early life in Kentucky. From Indian skirmishes to the kidnapping of Boone's daughter and the Calloway girls to the burgeoning lumber industry, the litany of the Bluegrass is celebrated in fine folk-art style. Remember to leave all glass containers, metal-detectors, and horses behind, but be sure to grab your cell phone if you want to listen to the recorded tour. By dialing (859) 592-9166 and following the prompts, you can hear messages about everything from building the fort to the old stone fences that populate the area.

At the far end of the parking lot, the wide, gravel trail begins its steady ascent to the earthwork fortification, erected on a high spot overlooking the Kentucky River. So yes, you have to hike up to the fort. But along the way are several interpretive signs describing everything from fort-building techniques to trees and flowers found in the vicinity. Add a liberal sprinkling of wooden benches, and everyone has plenty of opportunities to rest along the trail.

About a quarter of the way up the hill is a kiosk, with a visitor's log (it's always a good idea to sign in) and plenty of brochures free for the taking, including those promoting the beer cheese trail, stone fences of Kentucky, a historic walking tour of downtown Winchester, and so forth. But leave them for now, as you can always grab a few on your way back down.

The trail is mostly shaded by a variety of deciduous trees (and one particularly lovely mature paw paw tree if you are so lucky to be hiking in late summer.) As the trees give way to open fields, stop to admire the edge-type and turnpike dry-stone fences on your right, There's also a nice view of the river from here, although the towers of the Dale Power Station can prove distracting. There are also a half-dozen picnic tables just ahead, perfect for the school kids who visit.

The open field at the top of the hill showcases sweet blackberries, cornflower-blue chicory, and purple vetch in the summer, and wispy grasses and teasel in the fall. From here the trail circles around the earthen-berm fort, mimicking the ravens and turkey vultures circling overhead. Of course the views of the river are much better after the leaves have fallen, but so are the views of the power station and quarry operation, just upstream and downstream of Boonesborough, respectively.

Be sure to read about or listen to the cell phone tour message about the abatis ditch, found just below the earthen berm facing the river. If you see some neighborhood kids whittling sharp sticks one day, you might want to quickly grab some matches.

After filling your head with the details of the historical fort, close your eyes to better hear the roar of the breech and muzzle loaded guns and the sound of the canon firing. Smell the acrid smoke. Feel the earth tremble. Then saunter your way back down the hill to the wonders of the 21st century.

Note: Be sure you realize that this is an earthen berm fort and not a wood structure before you drag the kids up here. There are other earthwork forts at the Camp Nelson Civil War Heritage Park and the Leslie Morris Park at Fort Hill.

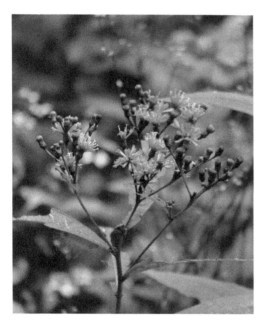

Side Trip:
Of course, if you've not been before (or it's been a very long time), you may want to walk around the older Fort Boonesborough. Although this park must be vying for one of the more poorly maintained state campgrounds in Kentucky, there are some very interesting historical sites worth checking out.

Civil War Fort at Boonesboro
1250 Ford Road (KY 1924)
Winchester, KY
Phone: (800) 298-9105
Web: civilwarfortatboonesboro.com

17 Clay Wildlife Management Area/Marietta Booth Tract

A multitude of hiking trails on nearly 7000 acres of less than pristine forested lands, snugged up against the banks of the Licking River.

Trail Length: 2 to 20+ miles

Facilities: None

Hours: Daily, sunrise to sunset.

Additional Information: Be sure to check the website for various hunting seasons. Obviously you don't want to be near this place in deer season. You should also avoid the area after heavy rains, as some of the well-worn horse trails become mud pits. The website has a decent topographic map that you can print out before you go.

Directions: From the intersection of I-75/64 and North Broadway, drive north on Paris Pike (US 27/68). Stay on US 68 all the way through downtown Paris and on to Millersburg. Once north of Millersburg, continue straight on KY 36 E, towards Carlisle. (KY 32 joins KY 36 in Carlisle.) Turn left on North Broadway Street towards Flemingsburg (KY 32 E). About 6 miles north of Carlisle, turn right on Cassidy Creek Road (KY 3315 / KY 57 S). There are two main entrances to Clay WMA, both on your left.

As a hiking destination, Clay WMA almost didn't make this book. On the plus side, the lay of the land is quite beautiful with multiple creek drainages and the Licking River providing the perfect ecosystem to support a variety of wildlife, wild flowers, and wild meanderings. Several boat ramps provide access to the Licking River and trails blanket the area. Deciduous hardwood forests cover much of the 7,000 acres, sporadically interrupted by open meadows, bounding deer, and turkey calls.

On the down side, by definition, a wildlife management area operates under an entirely different set of rules as compared to a park or a preserve. As a wildlife management area, Clay is open to hunters during various seasons (including multiple weekends) and horses have torn up several of the good trails. Unfortunately, some of the areas easily accessed by gravel road, including those close to the boat ramps, have been abused. Camping is free and few, if any, rules are enforced. The sad result is a scattering of beer cans, the occasional makeshift toilet, and just plain trash.

However, once you get away from the roads, the interior has some decent hiking, although we primarily recommend Clay WMA for those with some good orienteering skills, as trail signage remains elusive. Use a good compass to wind your way through the maze of trails not shown on the map. And be prepared for some good adventure, as you don't always end up where you think you will.

To access most of the hiking, take one of the two major gravel roads that leave Cassidy Creek Road on your left. Clay WMA Road (Lower Unit) is 2 miles from where you turned off KY 32 E. Clay WMA Road (Upper Unit) is almost 4 miles from where you turned off KY 32 E. A third option is to drive a little over 5 miles to Upper Lick Road and turn left. Another 3 miles of driving time will bring you to the Licking River and an abandoned bridge.

Turning left on Clay WMA Road (Lower Unit) takes you to several trails. One option is to begin at the boat ramp, hiking downstream (west) along the Licking River on the Grave Yard Trail. After hiking about 1 mile, the trail turns south and begins an upward climb. Another 1.5 miles brings you to a turn-around on a gravel road. Ignore the trash and find the second trail that heads back down the hill. In another mile you should connect back up with the Grave Yard Trail, for a total of 6 miles. This loop is not overly scenic, with the exception of the section along the river.

Another option is to take Clay WMA Road (Upper Unit) located 1.8 miles further down KY 3315. Bear right at the first Y, and then stay left. Park in the large turn-around. Pass through the gate and begin hiking the road north. Shortly a trail will come in on your right. This will lead you through a hardwood forest and in about three-quarters of a mile you will come across the place referred to as the Waterin' Hole. Continue left back up the hill and in about a mile you'll come to a large open field. Bearing right will take you to several spurs that follow various creek drainages to some beautiful spots along the Licking River. Alternately, turn left here and follow the road back to your vehicle.

While the Clay Wildlife Management Area falls short of pristine and stunningly beautiful hiking, it is less than 90 minutes from downtown Lexington and allows pets off leash. Outside of deer season and horse traffic, the area is lightly used. If paddling interests you, consider canoeing or kayaking the Licking River.

Side Trip:
Try the Marietta Booth tract just north of Clay WMA. Instead of turning off on KY 3315, continue on KY 32 for another 6.4 miles. Just after the small community of Cowan (at the RR tracks) take a right on Mooney Lane. You'll see signs for Marietta Booth. Although this 811-acre tract does not have any officially developed trails, there are several old farm roads that provide good views of the Licking River Valley and Fleming Creek (a major tributary of the Licking River). Neither horses nor ATVs are permitted on this land.

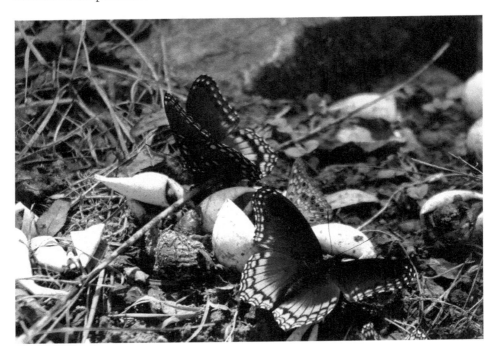

Clay Wildlife Management Area / Marietta Booth Tract
Cassidy Creek Road
Carlisle, KY 40311
Web: http://goo.gl/9NEPTN

18 Cove Spring Park and Nature Preserve

Hiking trails, natural springs, historical sites, and wetlands just a stone's throw from the distillery district of downtown Frankfort.

Trail Length: 0.3 to 6 miles

Facilities: Restrooms and drinking water available; picnic tables and shelters on a first-come basis.

Hours: 8 am until dusk.

Additional Information: Spring and early summer provide the best view of the creeks and wildflowers. Although trail signage is good, posted maps are inconsistent.

Directions: From the intersection of I-64 and US 60 (exit #58 on I-64), travel west on US 60 towards Frankfort for 2.5 miles. US 60 will turn left, but you want to keep going straight on KY 421 for another 1.5 miles. Exit on US 127 N, toward Owenton. Take an immediate right on Cove Spring Road. Follow park signs. To get to the wetlands portion of the park, stay on US 127 N for a few hundred feet, turning left into the parking lot.

Cove Spring has the unusual claim of being Frankfort's oldest and newest park. The springs located on the land served as the original source of drinking water for the city in the early 1800s and became popular for picnics and other social gatherings. However, the following century brought years of neglect as Frankfort's population grew and the city turned to the Kentucky River for its water supply. In the early 1990s, the parcel was bought by a private individual with the hope of preserving both the history and the ecosystem of the area. Soon after, the city of Frankfort bought the property and in 2002 it was reopened as a park.

Today Cove Spring is a mixture of history, hiking trails, wetlands preservation, picnic shelters, and the site of many workshops related to preserving our natural heritage. The 240-acre park is divided into two, with the main park located on the east side of US 127 and the wetlands portion on the western side of the road. Over 6 miles of hiking trails loop around the park, showcasing an excellent selection of native Kentucky plants and fauna.

Adjacent to the main parking lot you'll find an information kiosk with, among other things, a large map posted and smaller maps for the taking. However, the smaller maps are incomplete, as they do not show several of the newer trails. The more ambitious hiker might want to jot down a few notes from the larger posted map before heading out.

From the parking lot, 15-foot Hurst Falls will be to your right, with the trout raceway above it. Not to be confused with the Indy 500 for fins, a trout raceway is a man-made chute that carries fish from a stream to a calm pool below a waterfall. A stone dam and accompanying Kentucky River limestone overflow tower serve as historical focal points. Several smaller springs and cascading creeks are found throughout the park boundaries.

The quarter-mile Meadow Loop takes you to the Children's Memorial Garden (a touching and playful tribute) and to the Spring Spur Trail (the latter leading you to Cove Spring itself). Spring Spur, a third of a mile one-way, is as close to being a paved trail as one could get without actually being completely paved. Wide and flat, the walk is perfect for those with a slight shuffle to their gait or young children with boundless energy and little sense of direction.

The primary loop, the Holly Trail, can be combined with the Upland Trail for a scenic look at the heartlands of the park (counterclockwise provides the best tumbling creek views). The Osage Trail follows the outer boundaries of the park and will add about 2 more miles to your day.

Moving over to the wetlands side of the park (west of US 127) you will find an additional 2 miles of trails, including an old paved road, a short wooden walkway, and the wetlands path. The wetlands path is an elongated oval loop with two newly added spurs at the far end. There also is a trail map of the wetlands area posted on the information kiosk at this side of the park, and it differs yet again from other published maps. But hey…isn't this part of the adventure?

Side Trip:

Swing by Buffalo Trace Distillery (113 Buffalo Trace Way) for a free tour, which includes a bourbon tasting and chocolate bourbon balls. It's only minutes from Cove Spring Park. Tours run Monday-Friday, 9 am-3 pm; and Saturday, 10 am -2 pm.

Cove Spring Park and Nature Preserve
100 Cove Spring Road
Frankfort, KY 40601
Web: http://goo.gl/NKbuQM

19 Crutcher Nature Preserve

Ridge and meadow trail options, woodlands, creeks, and views of Kentucky palisades. Adjacent to Sally Brown Nature Preserve.

Trail Length: 2.8 miles; you can easily add another 2.5 miles from the trailhead.

Facilities: None

Hours: Daily, sunrise to sunset.

Additional Information: The first half-mile of the trail is less than spectacular, but becomes more scenic for those who persevere.

Directions: From Lexington, travel south on US 27 (Nicholasville Road), crossing the Kentucky River into Garrard County. At the top of the hill, turn right on KY 1845, also known as Rogers Road, the second road on the right after you cross the river. In 3.5 miles, KY 1845 Ts at the Camp Dick Fire Station. Turn left (on Polly's Bend Road) and travel 0.2 miles. Take a right at the stop sign on High Bridge Road. Go 2 miles and turn right on Bowman's Bottom Road. The road dead-ends on private property at the Bowman Brooks House. Park in the small gravel lot on your right.

The Crutcher Nature Preserve is one of three adjacent tracts owned and protected by The Nature Conservancy. This area is an excellent example of the success non-profits can have in protecting beautiful, yet fragile, ecosystems representative of our natural heritage. In conjunction with their partners, the Kentucky Chapter of The Nature Conservancy has protected over 40,000 acres across the state. Give often and give generously.

Inspired by the formation of the Sally Brown Nature Preserve, Dorothea Hillenmeyer Crutcher and her husband, Dr. Martin Crutcher created the preserve to celebrate their 50th wedding anniversary. We find it terribly romantic and take that as a challenge to other couples out there. According to the Nature Conservancy, this preserve protects "one of the largest concentrations of rare plant species in the Bluegrass."

The Crutcher Preserve is comprised of two separate tracts, together totaling 160 acres. The tract bordering the north side of the Kentucky River, in Jessamine County, is currently closed to the public. The tract adjacent to the Sally Brown Nature Preserve lies on the south side of the river (in Garrard County), and is bordered by other lands that are protected through conservation easement agreements. In tandem, these efforts work to protect an ecological area much larger than the Preserve itself.

Both the Crutcher and the Sally Brown Nature Preserves are serviced by the same parking lot and trailhead. Hikers can easily hike one trail system or the other, or hike them in combination. Each of the Preserves showcases some of the same wildflowers and hardwood forests indigenous to central Kentucky woodlands, and both offer spectacular views of the limestone cliffs or palisades towering over this section of the Kentucky River. However, each Preserve has its own unique sights and sounds, and personality to call its own.

To hike either the Crutcher or the Sally Brown Nature Preserves, directions to the trailhead are one in the same: After parking, pass through the fence at the end of the lot as indicated by the trail marker sign to the W.L. Lyons Brown Trail. Descend the hill by hugging the fence and tree line on your right, keeping the meadow to your left. A 75-yard perimeter walk will take you to another gate and another trail sign. Read the sign describing prescribed burning in the area and pass through the gate on your right. From there you will be able to see the kiosk, complete with brochures loaded in the mail box, topo maps, and a brief history of the area. Note the trail names and mileage markers. Pay homage to the young Girl Scout who graciously made this her merit project, and you're on your way.

The Crutcher Trail will be on your right and the W.L. Lyons Brown Trail (named after one of the generous benefactors of the Sally Brown Nature Preserve) will be to your left. (See the entry on the Sally Brown Nature Preserve for a complete description of the latter trail.) There are several options when hiking the Crutcher Trail: 1) straight out and around the loop and back to the kiosk; 2) hiking to Bowman's Bottom Road and back, alternating sides of the loop each way; 3) hiking to the road and then following the road back to the parking lot.

After leaving the kiosk, the first quarter mile of the Crutcher Trail is anticlimactic, particularly if you just hiked the Sally Brown. At this point you're wondering why you drove all the way out here. But keep walking. Soon you will be hiking ridge top, with views of the palisades off to your left (partially hidden in the summer months, but in clear view when the foliage has dropped). Multiple creeks dissect the trail, creating a perfect oasis for wildflowers in the springtime.

Reaching the loop trail gives you two choices: the trail to your left continues up river along the ridge line and can be the more interesting of the two, with views of the palisades and possible sightings of birds of prey. However, the path to your right soon leaves the forest canopy and borders a small meadow, which may allow for sightings of deer and bluebirds. The loops then meet again, and the spur to the road begins. At this point you can either return on the other side of the loop and hike back to the kiosk, or continue on the spur.

If you continue on the spur, you will soon pass a small meadow and the trail quickly drops down to another creek. As the trail sign indicates, cross over to the other side and begin hiking up the creek. (Do not cross the creek and hike up the other side.) Try not to walk in the creek itself any more than you must——it's better for the local inhabitants and keeps your boots dry. Soon you'll be marveling at the simplistic beauty of the millstone and speculating from where hence it came. If returning to the kiosk, this is a good place to stop. Otherwise, cross the creek once more, avoid falling into the sinkhole to your left, and keep the fenced-in meadow to your right. The gate is straight ahead, leaving you with a half-mile walk on the paved road back to the parking lot.

Crutcher Nature Preserve
Bowman's Bottom Road
Bryantsville, KY 40444
Web: http://goo.gl/zdCM2n

20 Dog Slaughter Falls

Make no bones about it. Despite its name, the water runs clear and sparkling.

Trail Length: 2.4 to 8 miles
Facilities: None available.
Hours: None posted.
Additional Information: Although dogs are permitted, keep your fingers crossed they can't read the map or trail signs.
Directions: Drive south on I-75. Take exit #25, Corbin. Follow US 25 W for 7.5 miles. Bear right on KY 90 W. Drive an additional 2.3 miles. Turn right on FR 195. The first trailhead will be less than one mile down this gravel road. Shoulder parking on the right; brown trail marker sign on your left. The second trailhead is 2 miles from the first TH. Shoulder parking and trailhead on your left.

This is a beautiful little gem of a hike, popular with locals and non-natives alike. Google *Dog Slaughter Falls* and thousands of images will pop up. Better yet, don't peak and go see for yourself. There are several stories circulating as to how the creek and falls got its name, none of them very pleasant and most highly imaginative. And rarely, if ever, do you see any of the explanations printed in tourism brochures.

Hikers have several options to hike Dog Slaughter Trail #414, which runs parallel to Dog Slaughter Creek. You can choose the upper trailhead, resulting in an 8-mile out-and-back hike; the lower trailhead, which reduces your hike to 2.4 miles round-trip; or a canine favorite, combining Bark Camp Creek and Dog Slaughter trails described below.

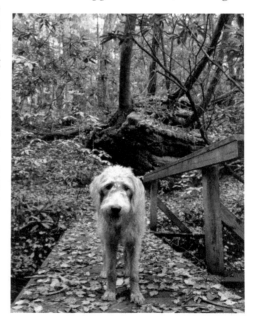

As you turn on FR 195, the first trailhead is not overly obvious, but look closely and you'll see the brown, wooden US Forest Service sign on your left. If you decide to start here, the trail immediately crosses Dog Slaughter Creek and stays on creek-left for 2.6 miles until you reach the second (downstream) trailhead. Note: the Forest Service mileage signs vary somewhat from actual GPS measurements, but not enough to worry about.

The upper section of the trail is quite nice as it follows the narrow creek through clouds of rhododendron and hemlock, occasionally giving way to beech, magnolia, paw paw, and spice bush if provided enough filtered sun-light. Here the creek murmurs quietly, like an intimate couple at a French cafe. However, the gravel road parallels the trail on the other side of the creek, so you do hear some noise from passing vehicles. During the week this is a rarity, but on a fine-looking Sunday afternoon the sound can be a little annoying. On the flip-side, you won't run into many people on the trail between the upper and lower trailheads. Using the upper trailhead access point, round-trip to the river and back will run you about 8 miles.

The second option is to take the second or lower trailhead, just above where Little Dog Slaughter Creek flows into its big brother. Park on the large left-hand

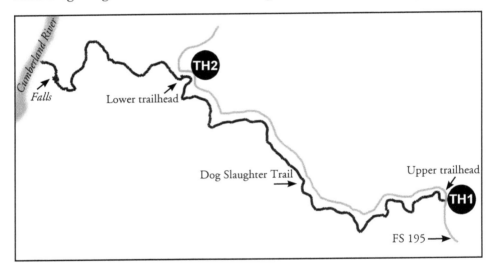

shoulder of the road and look towards the creek to find the trailhead. The trail soon crosses Dog Slaughter Creek and parallels the water on creek left. From here the gravel road bears north while you hike west, and peace and quiet becomes yours.

From the second trailhead, it's about 1.2 miles to Dog Slaughter Falls. Again, the trail along the creek passes under large hemlocks and through rhododendron thickets, as the water bubbles merrily away. Most of the creek is spring-fed, guaranteeing you a waterfall show year-round. But hands down, springtime after a heavy rain is a popular time to see the 15 to 20-foot falls.

Be sure to continue hiking the trail past the falls to where Dog Slaughter Trail ends at the Cumberland River. In less than 0.25 miles you will see a crooked white sign with red lettering, indicating that 5 miles further down the trail the Bark Camp Creek bridge is washed out. Given that the bridge was replaced in 2014, either the government lies, is uninformed or that the park system is simply underfunded. We prefer to believe the latter.

Turn right (north) at this sign and follow the short trail to a scenic bridge that spans Dog Slaughter Creek. At this point you could also head either north or south on the Sheltowee Trace Trail #100, as it follows the Cumberland River to add more mileage to your out-and-back hike.

Another option of hiking to Dog Slaughter Falls is from Cumberland Falls State Park. Follow the Moonbow Trail (a portion of the Sheltowee Trace) for three miles. Turn right (east) onto Dog Slaughter Trail. Hike a short distance to the falls. Round trip this option results in about 6.5 miles of hiking.

The last option to hike Dog Slaughter is a personal favorite, but requires running a 10-15 minute shuttle. You can string together Dog Slaughter, Sheltowee, and Bark Camp Creek trails (see the description elsewhere in this book) for an 8.6-mile hike.

Trail Map: http://goo.gl/mDY3xh

Side Trip: From either trailhead you are only 10-15 minutes to Cumberland Falls State Park. Wash up for dinner at the historic stone and log edifice known as DuPont Lodge and find a seat at one of the picture windows overlooking the river. After a hearty meal, stroll down to the falls and imagine what it would be like to run that big drop in an old whiskey barrel.

US Forest Service - London District
761 S. Laurel Road
London, KY 40744
Phone: (606) 864-4163
Web: http://goo.gl/ira2yP

21 Dupree Nature Preserve

One of three nature preserves found in Garrard County, Dupree is the newest effort to protect the rare flora and fragile ecosystems nestled in the Kentucky River Palisades region.

Trail Length: 4 miles, more or less

Facilities: Plastic outhouse.

Hours: Sunrise to sunset.

Additional Information: Sorry, pets are not permitted in nature preserves.

Directions: From the intersection of Man O' War and Nicholasville Road, in south Lexington, drive about 17.5 miles out Nicholasville Road (US 27 S), crossing the river into Garrard County. At the top of the hill, turn right on KY 1845 (aka Rogers Road). Drive 3.5 miles until the road ends at the Camp Dick Fire & Rescue Station. Turn right on Polly's Bend Road and drive 2.7 miles. Take the gravel road on your left into the parking lot.

Established, in part, with generous funding from Lexington businessman and former chairman of The Nature Conservancy Tom Dupree, this 300-acre preserve encompasses three miles of frontage along the Kentucky River known as Polly's Bend. Opened Oct. 5, 2013, the Dupree Nature Preserve is a work-in-progress battling invasive species (honeysuckle and winter creeper); developing rustic educational facilities for school children; and planting 12,000 native trees. Other improvements, including a new brick and mortar educational facility and restrooms, are on paper for future development.

The trails at Dupree provide excellent views of the 450-millon year old Ordovician limestone cliffs that tower over the river. Spring hikers will be rewarded with ample wildflower displays including yellow trout lilies, tooth-leaf cutwort, various rues and trilliums, May apple, and the striated leaves of putty root. It's not unusual to hear the maniacal cry of the pileated woodpecker or see birds of prey soaring overhead. Fall is also a good time to hike Dupree to enjoy the colors of the Chinquapin oak, beech, white ash, and yellowwood trees. Be sure to keep a sharp eye out for paw paws. During the winter, after the leaves have fallen, the views of the palisades are at their best and you're guaranteed to have the trails to yourself.

A nice 4-mile walk can be cobbled together from most of the trails in the preserve. The hike begins with an easy, but uneventful walk along a gravel path marked on preserve maps as the "Main Trail". After a mile, bear left on the 0.5-mile River Trail, which descends to an historic ferry crossing. Keep in mind that before the lock system was built, river levels were significantly lower, thus fording was much easier. Take some time watching the water flow past the small wooden dock and examining the old farm implements harking of a time long past.

Return back up the River Trail a short distance, until you see the Cliff Trail on your left. A steep 0.25-mile hike will bring you to the Overlook Trail for a clock-wise rotation. Turn left (north) on the Overlook Trail, as the dirt path threads between sinkholes of various sizes, including a few that, if filled with water, could easily hold all the staterooms of the QE2. Hikers will find a few nice benches scattered along the trail, just beckoning the company of a warm backside. The Overlook Trail will bring you back to the Main Trail. Bear left (east) to return to the parking lot.

A scavenger hunt is also available, using a list provided on-line from the Dupree Nature Preserve web site. Although there are both child and adult lists provided, most kids should be able to do both (and vice-versa!) Upload your pictures to receive free merchandise from The Nature Conservancy.

Scavenger hunt: http://goo.gl/4JrSsN

Trail Map: http://goo.gl/jXsKTh

Side Trip:
From Dupree Nature Preserve you are less than ten minutes to either the Sally Brown/ Crutcher or Dorman Nature Preserves. Pack a lunch and make a day of it doing the grand Garrard County river palisades circuit. See the description of these other preserves elsewhere in this book.

Once back home, sneak a peek at your investment portfolio. Perhaps one day you can give back to your community like Tom and his wife Ann Todd did. May we all be so lucky.

The Nature Conservancy of Kentucky
114 Woodland Avenue
Lexington, Kentucky 40502
Phone: (859) 259-9655
Web: http://goo.gl/r2zR4P

22 Eagle Falls

A short hike, with lots of steps, leading to several waterfall viewings.

Trail Length: 2.5 miles, with more mileage easily available.
Facilities: They have it all.
Hours: Trail closes at dark.
Additional Information: Sorry, pets are not permitted in nature preserves.
Directions: Driving south on I-75, take exit #25 in Corbin. Turn right on US 25 W, also heading south. Drive 7.4 miles. Make a slight right on KY 90 W. Drive a little over 8 miles. Go over the bridge which crosses the Cumberland River. The trailhead and parking area is just on your right.

How many of you have been to Cumberland Falls? The state resort park has just about everything...lodge, restaurant, swimming pool, campground, horseback rides...and for those into glamping, this is about as good as it gets.

But Cumberland Falls also has several really great hiking trails, including the one to Eagle Falls. While the trail can get quite busy during the summer and on beautiful fall/spring weekends, the hike also offers some incredible views of Cumberland Falls and wonderful wildflower displays.

The trailhead signs include some interesting information about the area and a map of the park. Most of the property around the falls is now a State Nature Preserve, meaning that there are extra trail rules to follow: No hunting; no pets; no picnicking. But the trade-offs for environmental protection are well worth the regulations.

Shortly after beginning the hike, you'll have excellent views of the Cumberland River and the horizon line that forms above the falls. Yes, it's a big drop here folks. The trail is quickly sandwiched between the riverbed on the right, and some really nice rockhouses and bluffs on your left. Be sure to note the huge tree burl next to the trail.

In about 0.3 miles, there is a short spur leading to what they call the Gorge Overlook. This is where you really begin to appreciate all the steps on this hike. There's an old CCC (Civilian Conservation Corps) hut built in the 1930s atop the ridge, with some partially obstructed views of the river valley below.

Returning back to the main trail, bear left and cross a small creek. On the other side of the drainage you will see a sign indicating the one-mile loop that lies ahead. To get to Eagle Falls, bear left here if you want to delay gratification or turn right if you're afraid someone might turn the water off.

Bearing left will take you along a small creek, past several pretty rock ledges, towering hemlocks, thickets of rhododendron and mountain laurel, and a profusion of spring wildflowers in season. The trail will then take you up and over a small ridge, as hollies, oaks, and magnolias become more prevalent. Almost immediately, the trail begins to descend again, along another small drainage. Be on the look-out for the trail blazes in the Michigan-fan colors of blue and bright yellow.

You'll soon be along Eagle Creek and views of two other smaller waterfalls. The quiet, placid creek belies the drop just ahead that forms Eagle Falls. But it will take you another 15-20 minutes of walking to work your way down to it.

At the next trail sign, bear left and take the short spur down to the river. The wood steps will give away to stone, before evolving into a long flight of black metal stairs. At the bottom, head downstream to the base of Eagle Falls. There are also several good views of Cumberland Falls from this vantage point.

After sufficient picture-taking, head back up the steps, bear left at the trail sign, and return to your vehicle. If you're hungry, there is a great picnic area just back across the bridge, on your right, and upstream of Cumberland Falls.

Trail Map: http://goo.gl/l5cal3

Side Trip:
If you're up for more hiking, the 5-mile Cumberland River Trail leaves from the picnic area mentioned above. The best segment is that portion that follows the Cumberland River.

Cumberland Falls State Resort Park
7351 Highway 90
Corbin, KY 40701
Phone: (606) 528-4121
Web: http://parks.ky.gov/parks/resortparks/cumberland-falls/

23 Elkhorn Creek Nature Trail at Great Crossing

A shorter trail, perfect for those wanting to escape into the wilderness, but just not too far.

Trail Length: 3 miles (round-trip)
Facilities: Picnic pavilion, small boat ramp, port-a-potty. No water.
Hours: No hours posted.
Additional Information: Posted: *No profanity or gambling permitted.* (No kidding.) Be wary of encroaching suburbs.

Directions: From the Scott County courthouse (at the intersection of US 460 and US 25), head west on US 460. Just past Western Elementary School, turn right on KY 227 N. Travel 0.3 miles, and then take a right into the park.

Where else can you hear cattle lowing and men shouting 'fore!'? See sycamore branches larger than the thighs of a lineman for the Green Bay Packers? Stroll past kingfishers, swimming holes, and Kentucky sliders (turtles that is; not White Castle burgers)?

This 1.5-mile trail connects Great Crossing Park on Elkhorn Creek with Western Elementary School. Access at Western is limited to those days when the school is not in session, so it may be easier to just park at the Park and start from there.

Parking is easy, with a picnic pavilion, port-a-potty, and boat ramp readily available. Bring your own drinking water. The trail leaves the far end of the lot, next

to a large, dilapidated information board filled with mud dauber nests and spider webs. Follow the asphalt-paved path for approximately 50 yards, balancing the Elkhorn on your left and open fields on your right.

Be sure to keep your eyes open for wild critters, both high and low. About midway you'll pass one of the largest burr oaks in central Kentucky. Several other trees have been adorned with short sections of 2x4s, leading up to swinging ropes hanging midstream. A small fishing boat or two will almost always keep you company as you follow the creek.

After a half-mile walk, you'll cross a small wooden bridge. If steps are a concern, take a right and climb the hill towards the black metal gate. Otherwise, continue on through the lightly wooded area until you see the wooden handrail on your right. The steps take you away from the creek, along an old stone fence. Another 5-10 minutes of walking will bring you alongside a private golf course on your left, with open fields on your right.

Once the trail becomes asphalt again, you should be in sight of Western Elementary. The paved trail continues along the backside of the school, vaguely loops around, and returns back to the path again. Backtrack to your vehicle and you've done 3 miles.

A big plus for some hikers is pets are permitted as long as they are under control (which is obviously open to interpretation). There is no mention of leashes for kids, although for some that may be a requirement. This trail is a good way to stretch your legs after a few hours of canoeing or fishing from the shore. Bring a picnic lunch and game of checkers for sitting under the pavilion on a hot sultry day.

Side Trip:
After leaving the park, turn right on KY 227 N. In a few miles you'll come to the small town of Stamping Ground, named after the large herds of bison that used to roam these parts as they traveled along the Great Buffalo Trace. The bison would stop to drink at Buffalo Spring, which the town has since turned into a small park with a picnic shelter. The town was also the marriage site for the parents of Frank and Jesse James. Now that's trivia!

Elkhorn Creek Nature Trail at Great Crossing Park
Stamping Ground Road (KY 227)
Georgetown, KY 40324

24 Floracliff Nature Sanctuary

Cross over one of the largest known surface deposits of travertine rock that forms Elk Lick Falls, as you make your way to meet Woody C. Guthtree——the oldest documented tree in all of Caintuck.

Trail Length: 3 to 5 miles

Facilities: Nature center, bathrooms, drinking water.

Hours: Guided tours and by appointment only. Nature center is open during guided tours only.

Additional Information: No solo excursions.

Directions: From the intersection of Richmond Road and Man O' War Blvd., continue east on Richmond Road (US 25/421) for about 1.6 miles. Turn right on Old Richmond Road (just across from Jacobson Park), staying on US 25/421. After another 6 miles, Old Richmond Road will go over I-75 and you'll see Grimes Mill Road on your left. Immediately after that, turn right on Elk Lick Falls Road (taking you back under I-75), and then an immediate left to stay on Elk Lick Falls Road. Floracliff will be another 2 miles on your right.

Part of the ever-growing collection of Kentucky state nature preserves, Floracliff was founded by Dr. Mary Wharton, our very own wildflower maven, author, and benefactress. A new nature center provides a beautiful starting point for many group tours and outdoor classroom adventures on almost 5 miles of trails throughout the 287-acre sanctuary.

Hiking the sanctuary requires advance reservations, and uninvited trespassers may be shot and hung for the turkey vultures to feast upon. Keep an eye on their (Floracliff's, that is) website for posted hikes scheduled throughout the year. Typically 3 to 4 guided hikes are offered each month and a simple old-fashioned phone call reserves your place. By design, the trails at Floracliff are unmarked and maps are unavailable.

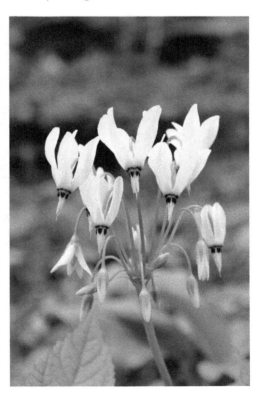

After leaving the nature center, a woodland trail leads you to the merger of Kettle Springs Branch and Falls Creek Branch before the water tumbles down a huge chunk of calcium carbonate, known in geologic circles as travertine rock, forming Elk Lick Falls. A short distance away, Woody (circa 1611) stands with the chubby arms of an aged Chinquapin oak, wondering who will write on the wall of his very own Facebook page. Groundwater and natural springs provide nourishment for the harbingers of spring, including shooting stars, Virginia bluebells, poppies, and trillium.

Floracliff takes its education outreach responsibilities seriously, offering a variety of guided walks for school children, hands-on workshops, and environmental activities designed for the classroom. Various research projects are jointly pursued with outside entities. Opportunities abound for those wishing to take out their aggression on the bush honeysuckle, which is more prevalent than the freckles on Opie Taylor's upturned nose.

Side Trip:
On the way back to Lexington, stop at Jean Farris Winery, 6825 Old Richmond Road. You can sit on their patio, select a little something from their extensive wine collection, and contemplate how to get new sources of funding for nature preserves.

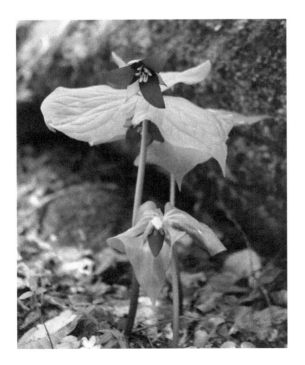

Floracliff Nature Sanctuary
8000 Elk Lick Falls Road
Lexington, KY 40515
Phone: (859) 351-7770
Web: floracliff.org

25 Griffith Woods Wildlife Management Area

A glimpse back in time at the savanna-woodland habitat of the central Bluegrass Region.

Trail Length: 1 mile and more.
Facilities: None available.
Hours: Open daily, dawn to dusk.
Additional Information: Please read the wildlife management area section near the back of this book. WMAs have limited hunting seasons and it's good for everyone to know the rules. Dogs permitted.
Directions: From Lexington, head north on Russell Cave Road (KY 353). Twenty miles outside of New Circle Road, KY 353 runs into US 62. Bear right (north) on US 62 E. In a few blinks of an eye, on your right is a small, unmarked entrance to Griffith Woods. Park in the gravel lot. A second entrance is just north of the first, but on the left side of the road.

Formerly known as Silver Lake Farm, Griffith Woods protects some of the giant chinquapin oaks, burr oaks, and blue ash that first set root here 150 to 350 years ago. This 746-acre parcel of land safeguards one of the remaining examples of the open woodland habitat that covered most of central Kentucky.

Don't expect well-developed trails here or even neatly mowed paths. Instead, the old fields continue to be outlined with bush hogging lanes, accented with a proliferation of deer tracks. If you suffer from a weak sense of direction, you may want to bring a compass (or smart phone) along, so you can find your way back to your vehicle. But it would be a stretch to get lost at Griffith Woods, as the grass blades clearly outnumber the tree trunks.

After parking at the first entrance, head southeast from the gravel lot to find a patchwork of fields, a few dilapidated farm buildings, and an aging barn in fairly good shape. Feel free to roam and discover things on your own accord. Meander around the old pastures where lavender-colored thistles, black-eyed Susans, purple and white asters, cornflower-blue chicory, and delicate Queen Anne's lace dot the fields. It's like having your very own farm without having to repair the fence-lines or pay the taxes.

But if you're anxious to find the ancient ones, head towards the southern side of the farm. Many of the centuries-old trees can be found adjacent to the mowed paths. In addition to the revered oaks and ash, walnuts, hickories, and locusts abound here, providing mast for the wildlife that call this place home.

So how do we tell the age of a tree? Most of us are familiar with counting the annual growth rings to determine a tree's age. Unfortunately that's really difficult to do with a live specimen. Ditto for more modern techniques such as MRI-style scans. An increment borer could also be used to extract a core sample, but that might open the tree up to disease, insects, and rot.

However, there are several simple mathematical formulas used to calculate a tree's age using specie-specific growth factors and tree trunk diameter measurements. Further, as a tree matures, its trunk and limbs begin to show signs of its age such as stubby arms, huge burls, weather damage, and pronounced bark characteristics. If only these giants could talk.

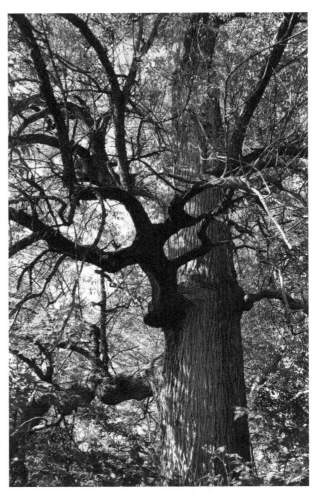

Note: The web site for Friends of Griffith Woods currently includes some out-of-date information, suggesting that the area is not open to the public, except by appointment. However, the Kentucky Department of Fish and Wildlife Resources now owns the farm. Otherwise the web site includes some valuable and interesting information about this landmark. Please see friendsofgriffithwoods.org.

Griffith Woods WMA
Kentucky Department of Fish and Wildlife Resources
#1 Sportsman's Lane Frankfort, KY 40601
Phone: (859) 428-2262
Web: http://goo.gl/J1E8ca

26 Hisle Park

Open fields, open skies.

Trail Length: 3.5 miles

Facilities: Picnic area, water, plastic outhouse.

Hours: November 1 - April 31, 8 am-5 pm. Otherwise 8 am to dusk.

Additional Information: Dogs are permitted on leash, but please clean up after them. Mountain biking is not permitted. Please yield to horses by walking on the right and passing to your left.

Directions: From Lexington, head east on Bryan Station Road. About 2 miles past the I-75 overpass, turn right on Briar Hill Road. Drive a little over a mile. The address is 3551 Briar Hill Road. Hisle Park will be on your left.

As far as Lexington goes, this is one of our more unusual parks, primarily because there's not much out there. Designed for hikers and equestrian riders, the old Hisle farm has been converted to a rural park of sorts. LFUCG describes it perfectly: 280 acres of rolling pastureland. The land was deeded to the city in 1989, which has future plans for expanding the trails, developing an orchard, building a pavilion, and stocking the ponds.

The trails loop in and out of open fields, occasionally intersecting with an old tree line or skimming past a small pond. From the parking area, Trail Loop A winds west of the barn for about a mile. Trail Loop B does the same thing east of the barn for 2.5 miles. The mornings and early evenings are the nicest out here, and cross-country snow skiing can be had in the winter. Not many equestrians use the mowed paths and care has been taken not to ride when it's muddy, which can be quite damaging to the trails.

Side Trip:
If you drive just a wee bit further to 3655 Briar Hill Road, you come to the second "half" of Hisle Park which has Lexington's only archery range open to the public. You're free to use the permanent targets or bring your own. Every young girl will want to channel her own inner Katniss.

Hisle Park Equestrian Trails
3551 and 3655 Briar Hill Road
Lexington, KY 40516
Web: http://goo.gl/F4e0eW

27 Jim Beam Nature Preserve

A one-mile loop through an uneventful lightly wooded area of early successional native evergreens (primarily cedar); however, the spring wildflower show may be worth the drive.

Trail Length: 1 mile

Facilities: None available.

Hours: Daily, sunrise to sunset.

Directions: From Lexington, head south on Nicholasville Road. Travel approximately 15.6 miles south of Man O' War Blvd, passing Camp Nelson National Cemetery on your left and the gray barrack-style distillery warehouses of Jim Beam on your right. Turn right on Hall Road. Go up the hill and through the 4-way stop. Turn right on Payne Lane. The paved road will make a sharp turn to the right; proceed straight ahead on the gravel road. If the gate at the bottom of the hill is closed, park immediately on your left, adjacent to the cemetery. (Note: The gate is frequently closed and is no indication that the preserve is actually closed.)

The Jim Beam Nature Preserve encompasses 115 acres along some of the palisades, or limestone cliffs, formed by the Kentucky River. The land was donated to the Nature Conservancy in 1995 in celebration of Jim Beam's 200th anniversary. Some of the bourbon-drinking aficionados amongst our readers might know that Jim Beam is one of the top selling bourbons in the world.

Planning your foray to Jim Beam Nature Preserve for the winter and early spring months may afford the hiker the best views of the palisades. The area also has a high concentration of rare plant species, including many wildflowers, and offers an excellent research environment for invasive species including Chinese privet and bush honeysuckle.

At the end of the gravel parking area, pass through the fence to gain entrance to the trail. A short walk will bring you to the top of a loop. Travel either direction, although the signage is a bit clearer when traveling counterclockwise.

Before entering the loop, you will also pass a large meadow on your right, heavily populated with cedars. As a trial project for invasive species control, the Nature Conservancy occassionally permits the free cutting of cedars during the Christmas season. It is here you will also find a large sign honoring "2000 in 2000", a tree-planting project sponsored by the Jim Beam company.

Depending on gas prices, it may not be worthwhile to drive this far for a one mile trail. If a spring remains in your step, drive on to one of the other three hiking areas in close proximity to Jim Beam (the Tom Dorman, Sally Brown, or Crutcher State Nature Preserves) to see more of the palisades and central Kentucky woodlands. Alternately, if the day is cold, you may want to retire to the comfort of your living room, with a smooth glass of bourbon in one hand and a good book in the other.

Side Trip:

For the history buffs in your group, stop by the small white chapel you passed on Hall Road (on your left as you leave the area). The church property was the former site of the "Refugee School" known variously as the Ariel Academy, Camp Nelson Academy, or Ariel College. (The community of Hall was originally known as Ariel.) John Fee, the founder of Berea College, was instrumental in the establishment of the school to serve the families of the high number of colored troops who served at Camp Nelson during the Civil War. The school opened around 1865 and operated for 50 years as an educational institution for both African-American and white children in an equalitarian effort to integrate the races.

Jim Beam Nature Preserve
Payne Layne
Hall, KY 40444
Web: http://goo.gl/7BzH2Y

28 John A. Kleber Wildlife Management Area

Multiple trail and off-trail opportunities including hiking and fishing within the woodlands of central Kentucky.

Trail Length: 4.4 to 7.6 miles
Facilities: None available.
Hours: Daily, sunrise to sunset.
Additional Information: Check the website for deer hunting season. Some four-legged critters wear radio-controlled collars.
Directions: From the intersection of New Circle Road and Georgetown Street, continue heading north on Georgetown, which later becomes Lexington Road or US 25. Drive 8.3 miles, then turn left on US 460 W Bypass / US 62. After another 2.7 miles, turn left on US 460. In a little over 0.5 miles, take a right on KY 227. Travel 8.1 miles, then bear left on KY 368 or Cedar Road. Finally, after another 7.3 miles you'll see a gravel road on your right, framed with a bright yellow gate that takes you to a small gravel parking lot.

With over 2300 acres, Kleber WMA has lots of room to roam. The most easily recognized trail begins just off Cedar Creek Road, accessed using the directions provided above. After parking, step over the cable gate and head down the old roadbed. The trail meanders along the Elm Fork of Cedar Creek, crossing through cedar thickets and deciduous hardwood forest.

The trail is fairly flat, with only two noticeable "hills" worth mentioning. After walking about 1.6 miles you'll descend the second hill and rejoin Elm Fork on your right. Beaver activity will become increasingly obvious and at low water you'll see a second trail crossing the stream and scrambling up the other side. You now have two choices.

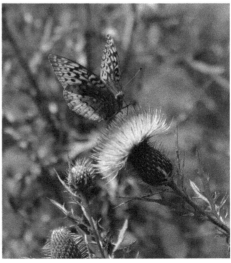

If the water is too high or your boots are getting too wet, you can continue on the creek side path another one-half mile or so until you reach the shooting range off Harmony Road (accessed from the other side of Kleber). Unless

Harmony Rd.

Shooting Range

TH

gravel road

Elm Fork of Cedar Creek

KY 368

Cedar Rd. (KY 368)

you've run a shuttle, your best option is to turn around and backtrack to your vehicle. The distance from the trailhead to the shooting range is 2.2 miles or 4.4 miles round-trip.

If you decide to brave the stream, the trail continues south another 1.6 miles to Oakland Branch Road. To cross the stream, you can walk atop the small beaver dam built of rocks, sticks, and mud. Just upstream of the dam, the trail follows an old abandoned roadbed up to the top of a ridge. While this potion of the trail can get somewhat overgrown, it is clearly marked with red and white horse signs.

The trail clears out on top of the ridge, leaving you with a beautiful walk through central Kentucky woodlands, passing an old stone foundation on your left and a vernal pool on your right. Here oaks, hickories, and ash trees abound. About 1.1 miles from the creek, the old dirt road ducks under a red metal gate, before turning to gravel. Another half-mile takes you to a yellow metal gate and Oakland Branch Road. From the creek to the paved road it is 1.6 miles one-way (3.2 miles round-trip). If you combine the creek side trail to the shooting range and the ridge top trail to Oakland Branch Road, you have hiked 7.6 miles in total.

These two trails only scratch the surface as to what is available at Kleber. The area is crisscrossed with old roads and game trails. Wildlife is plentiful, including deer, turkey, duck, and other small mammals. Kleber is also the site of the annual Christmas Bird Count conducted by the Frankfort Audubon Society and the Frankfort Bird Club.

Side Trip:
On your way back to Stamping Ground, take either Snavely or Switzer Road and head over to the old Switzer covered bridge, located on Elkhorn Creek, at the intersection of KY 1262 and KY 1689. Grab the camera and listen for the clop of horse hooves from yesteryear.

John A. Kleber Wildlife Management Area
KY 368 (Cedar Creek Road)
Owenton, KY 40359
Web: http://goo.gl/ETmd0V

29 John B. Stephenson Memorial Forest State Nature Preserve

Anglin Falls…a beautiful gem south of Berea.

Trail Length: 2 miles roundtrip

Facilities: None available.

Hours: Daily, sunrise to sunset.

Additional Information: The best time to visit may be spring, which provides a spectacular wildflower display and waterfall show.

Directions: Please READ this. Several versions are available on the Internet, with varying degrees of accuracy. From Lexington, head south on I-75. Take exit #76, traveling 1.5 miles east on KY 21, to downtown Berea. You then have two options:

Option One: Continue straight on KY 21 for another 5 miles until it Ts into US 421. Turn right on US 421. Go up Big Hill for 2.7 miles. Just after you cross into Rockcastle County and the right lane ends, turn right on Burnt Ridge Road (KY 1046). Drive 0.2 miles, and then take a left on Hammonds Fork. Drive another 3.4 miles and take a sharp left turn on Anglin Falls Road. After 0.9 miles, you will see a red and white sign on your left that says 'Anglin Falls,' posted to a black mailbox (#842). If you're lucky, a field of llamas will be in the pasture on your right. Shortly, the road ends in a small parking area at the trailhead.

Option Two: Once in downtown Berea, turn right at the stop sign (KY 1617, also known as KY 595 or Scaffold Cane Road). Drive 4.9 miles. KY 1617 veers right, Burnt Ridge Road goes left, and you want to go straight on KY 1787 or Davis Branch Road. Another 2.4 miles and you'll be looking at the old Disputanta Post Office. Turn left on Hammonds Fork Road (known on some maps as Himanns Fork). Go another 0.85 miles and then take a sharp right on Anglin Falls Road. After 0.9 miles, you will see a red and white sign on your left that says 'Anglin Falls,' posted to a black mailbox (#842). If you're lucky, a field of llamas will be in the pasture on your right. Shortly, the road ends in a small parking area at the trailhead.

This 123 acres of Kentucky hardwood forest was a memorial gift in 1996 from the friends of John B. Stephenson (long-time President of Berea College) and Friends of Anglin Falls. We wish more of us had friends like that. The Preserve encompasses Anglin Creek and the small gorge it created.

The trail begins on relatively flat terrain, blanketed with luscious ground cedar on either side, and sprinkled with many of the 32 varieties of ferns found in the area. You will cross Anglin Creek once and depending on recent rainfall, two or more smaller creeks tumbling down the steep hillsides. The path gradually climbs higher before scrambling over large moss- and lichen-covered boulders of aggregate rock. Just remember, the wetter your boots the more magnificent the almost 75' waterfall will be at the far end of the trail.

The occasional bench provides a good excuse to observe the towering yellow poplars, maples, and oaks. Spring gives rise to wood poppies, hepatica, wild columbine, putty root, toothwort, and catchfly, to name a few. Proximity to the falls will be marked with a larger number of rocky outcroppings, hemlocks, and the sound of dripping, gurgling water. You can stop at the base of the falls or scramble up many of the winding paths for a view from higher up. The only thing this trail doesn't have is length, but it provides true testimony that good things do come in small packages.

Anglin Falls

Anglin Falls Road

TH

Side Trip:
If you are looking for a full day of liquid wonder, this hike could easily serve as an adjunct to the Waterfall Chasing entry found in this book. Or you could add Anglin Falls onto hiking at Berea College Forest. Option One driving directions pass directly by the Pinnacles trailhead.

**John B. Stephenson Memorial
Forest State Nature Preserve**
Anglin Falls Road
Conway, KY 40456
Web: http://goo.gl/JPwzrc

30 Leslie Morris Park at Fort Hill

The park is both a Civil War historic site and hiking area that overlooks downtown Frankfort.

Trail Length: 0.6 to 4.8 miles

Facilities: Bathrooms and drinking water are available only during Visitor Center hours.

Hours: The grounds are open sunrise to sunset. Closed Christmas, New Year's Day, and Thanksgiving. The Visitors Center is open Tuesday-Saturday, 11 am–5 pm, from Memorial Day to Halloween (yes… that's what the sign says.) Free guided tours Monday - Saturday, Memorial Day to Oct. 31.

Directions: From the intersection of I-64 and US 60 (exit 58 on I-64), travel west on US 60 towards Frankfort for 2.5 miles. US 60 will turn left, but you want to keep going straight on KY 421 for another 1.5 miles. Exit on KY 127 S, toward Frankfort. Drive 0.5 miles on KY 127 (Holmes Street), turning right on Henry Street. At this point you'll begin to see signs for Fort Hill Park. Take an almost immediate left on Hillcrest Avenue; drive another 0.3 miles before veering right on Clifton. Pass through the large black iron gates.

This 124-acre park truly has a little something for everyone. Civil War history buffs will enjoy the remains of two earthwork forts, guided tours, and living history programs. Families with young children will appreciate some of the paved hiking trails. And those disgruntled with state government can hoof it up Old Military Road to blow off some steam and clear their heads.

Those interested in the fort itself may want to go straight to the Sullivan House, which serves as the Visitor Center for the park. Originally a two-story log house, with a dogtrot down the middle, you can get an overview of the fort's history and a taste of early 19th century life in Kentucky. Although the tours are free, the tour guides are worth their weight in Civil War gold coins.

From the Sullivan House you can take a self-guided walking tour of the remains of the earthwork forts, much of which is accessible via paved trails. The park also has a wheelchair available for those wishing to cruise their way back through time. A good view of the state capitol can be seen from the overlook.

The park's hiking system can be accessed from near the Sullivan House or from the small parking lot on your right soon after entering the park. Information kiosks with trail maps are available at both sites. The 0.6-mile Miller Trail is a paved asphalt loop that connects to both the Goin Trail (a 0.75-mile wood-chip path) and the 0.2-mile Cave Loop Trail. For those wanting to get more vertical, take the Old Military

Road trail that runs all the way to Kentucky River View Park behind Capital Tower Plaza in downtown Frankfort. Then run all the way back up again.

Prior to the formation of the park in 1999, the land had been farmed until the 1960s. Consequently, much of the woods are relatively new growth with an abundance of cedar, locusts, osage orange, and black cherry. However, oaks and maples are making their presence known. To the parks credit, significant efforts are being made to preserve the area for wildlife. However, the resident herd of white-tailed deer, frequently seen by visitors, has overgrazed the park.

Side Trip:
The Zeigler House is the only Frank Lloyd Wright residence in the state of Kentucky. Wright met Reverend Jessie R. Zeigler while on a ship in route to Europe. The meeting must have gone well, since Wright received a commission to build what is referred to as the "Fireproof House for $5,000" in Wright's prairie-house style. Since Wright was in Europe, his colleagues actually designed the house. Built in 1910, the private residence can be seen at 509 Shelby Street.

Leslie Morris Park at Fort Hill
400 Clifton Avenue
Frankfort, KY 40601
Phone: (502) 696-06070
Web: http://goo.gl/mrV40l

31 Lick Creek and Princess Falls

Waterfalls, wildflowers, rockhouses, and boulder-choked creeks——what else could one want in a trail?

Trail Length: 8 miles out-and back (4 miles one-way).

Facilities: None and we like it that way.

Hours: None posted.

Additional Information: Dogs are permitted off-leash.

Directions: Drive south on I-75. Take exit #62 (US 25) south towards KY 461. Follow KY 461 for 18 miles. Bear right (west) on KY 80 for 6 miles. Take a left on KY 914 and drive for another 4.5 miles.

Turn left on KY 1247 and go for 4 miles. Merge onto US 27 S. Follow US 27 south for about 23 miles to Whitley City. Turn right (west) on KY 478. Almost immediately, turn left (south) on KY 1651. Notice the Dairy Bar on your right. Drive less than a mile. Turn right on Ranger Station Road (the first paved road past the school bus garage.) Parking is immediately on your right, by the kiosk. Trailhead will be on your left.

This is a great hike any time of the year. Spring rains gather in the creeks producing gorgeous waterfalls. Rockhouses stay cool in the heat of summer. Fall brings autumnal colors to the sassafras, beech, and oaks. And winter promises icy stalactites and quiet solitude. Just don't tell too many people about this place though. Even a lot of the locals haven't been here.

The first mile of trail follows an old logging road, which promises both blueberries in mid-summer and hungry ticks all season long. But this ridgetop hike won't last long as the trail begins descending into the Lick Creek drainage. Two sets of metal stairs and another quarter-mile of hiking will bring you to the base of several really great rockhouses.

After crossing a small tributary, the trail runs adjacent to Lick Creek. Even at low water levels the two- and three-story high rocks lodged in the creek bed create interesting hydraulics and sounds. In the spring and mid-summer, the wildflowers along Lick Creek can be gorgeous. In particular, the area hosts a nice display of lady slippers and mountain laurel.

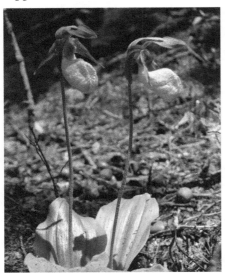

About two miles from the trailhead, on your left you will see the half-mile spur to Lick Creek Falls. The trail follows a small tributary of Lick Creek that fools one into underestimating the power and the beauty of the waterfall that lies ahead. Give thanks to the previous trail builders who laid the beautiful stones defining the trail, as it winds beneath more rock overhangs and shelters. Even in winter, the water seeps and the icicles drip from the huge rockhouse formed by the falls. An awesome lunch spot awaits you at the beach formed by the continual erosion of the sandstone overhang that began many millennia ago.

Trace your steps back to the main trail, turning left when you rejoin Lick Creek. There is a shortcut down an old trail, but if you're uncertain you can easily backtrack all the way back to the original junction. Either way, bear left (west) on the Lick Creek Trail. Be prepared for several creek crossings, which in early spring can be rather challenging. In less than a mile you will approach Princess Falls from the upstream side.

Following the trail on creek-left, you'll see a short spur leading below the waterfall. Whereas Lick Creek Falls is a plunge-style waterfall, Princess is more block-style and forms a curtain as it falls off the bedrock. Even at low water levels, the spring-fed creek continues to create a nice show here and at higher levels Princess Falls is a solid sheet of falling water. Although there is a sweet camping spot just below the falls on creek-right, try and refrain from camping within 300 feet of the stream.

If you want, continue the last 0.2 miles down Lick Creek Trail to the bridge where it joins the Sheltowee Trace, just a short distance from the Cumberland River. Turning left (west) on the Sheltowee will take you to KY 92 and a right (north) will take you towards the Yahoo area and a really cool set of bridges at Negro Creek. Unless you have run shuttle, just retrace your steps back to the trailhead.

Side Trip:
Remember passing the Dairy Bar? After hiking, head back into Whitley City for homemade milkshakes, burgers, and pie-in-a-cup, all served in authentic 1950s regalia. They will even take your orders outside if you're too dirty and/or fragrant to be caught on the inside. The Dairy Bar, 198 S. Main Street. (606) 376-2124. Closed on Sundays; but Milton's Burger Hut on US 127 will be open.

Trail Map:
http://goo.gl/RxZCwn

Stearns Ranger District
3320 Hwy. 27 North
Whitley City, KY 42653
Phone: (606) 376-5323

32 Lower Howard's Creek Nature and Heritage Preserve

A glowing gem working hard to protect endangered plant species and remnants of yesteryear.

Trail Length: 2 to 5 miles of trail and a lifetime of story telling.

Facilities: No water, bathrooms, or t-shirt shops on the premises.

Hours: The Holder Trail is open daily, sunrise to sunset. The rest of the Preserve is open for scheduled tours only. See their website for organized hikes.

Additional Information: No pets allowed. Children are welcome on guided hikes if accompanied by a responsible adult.

Directions: Drive east on Richmond Road, KY 418 E. From where Richmond Road crosses I-75 (exit 104), follow Athens-Boonesboro Rd. (KY 418 E). The main Preserve entrance (scheduled tours only) is located 7.4 miles east of I-75, on the left side of the road. The Holder Trail is located about 0.5 miles past the main Preserve entrance, or about 8 miles east of I-75, on the left side of the road and behind Hall's on the River Restaurant.

According to local lore, stone fences must be built horse high, bull strong, or hog tight. Here at Howard's Creek you'll find all three. Throw in some wonderful story telling and you have the woman who manages the Preserve in her Blundstone-boot good looks and country-drawl sharp wit. We need more nature preserves like this.

The Preserve lies along both sides of Lower Howard's Creek, buffeted by a small limestone gorge on either side. Begin by checking out their website and reserving a spot on the popular guided day hikes ranging from 1-4 hours. Of course, if you have a desire to pull honeysuckle, sign up for a few volunteer hours and you'll have your workout, too.

An extension of the original Wilderness Road rambles across the 358 acres that comprises the main part of the Preserve. Over 5 miles of trails follow the old roadbed, which cuts across open meadows, tumbles along Trimble Creek, hugs old stone fence lines and brushes against several historical sites. The swinging bridge carries you across Lower Howard's Creek to the remains of an 1800s gristmill, stone house, cooper's shack and meat house.

If you decide to join one of the guided hikes you won't be disappointed. For a suggested $5 donation you'll hear a lively commentary of local politics, wildflower identification and ancillary discussions, such as the use of sister joists to shore up old floors. Part of the Kentucky State Nature Preserve system, many of the plants and wildflowers are endangered or threatened, and two of the building sites are listed on the National Register of Historic Places.

Alternately, you may choose to hike the John Holder Trail, which is free and open to the public. Park behind Hall's restaurant and follow the trail that leaves from the side road which leads to the back parking lot. Near the small signpost are brochures if you have not already printed one out. The brochure is filled with interesting historical tidbits about the area and some of the ruins along the trail. Be sure to read on the web-site about the triple murder at the Downey House.

Touted as one of the first true entrepreneurs of Central Kentucky, Colonel Holder developed a commercial-industrial area in 1782 where Lower Howard's Creek flows into the Kentucky River. The early settlement included a ferry, store, tavern, boatyard, warehouse and mill. Remarkably, Holder was able to accomplish all of this without any tax-increment financing or tungsten carbide drill bits.

Side Trip:

After leaving the Preserve, continue on KY 418 just a few more miles until you see the Kentucky River. Skip a few rocks and imagine shipping all your supplies along this ancient waterway. For classic Kentucky fare, grab a table at Hall's On the River, 1225 Athens-Boonesboro Road for some homemade beer cheese and lamb fries. If the weather is cooperative, the porch overlooking the creek is just about perfect.

Lower Howard's Creek Nature and Heritage Preserve

1945 Athens-Boonesboro Road
Winchester, KY 40391
Phone: (859) 744-4888
Web: lowerhowardscreek.org

33 Masterson Station Park

Grass path and shared-use trails straddling one of Lexington's largest city parks and a fascinating history few residents know about.

Trail Length: 4.5 miles

Facilities: Picnic tables, soccer fields, horse jumps, cross-country race trails, and a dog park. Water and bathroom facilities are available seasonally.

Hours: Daily, sunrise to sunset.

Additional Information: The open fields can be quite windy and the creekside trails rather wet after heavy rains.

Directions: From Lexington, travel northwest on Leestown Road. About 2 miles outside of New Circle Road, turn right on Ruffian Way and into Masterson Station Park (just past the subdivision of the same name.)

Most Lexingtonians know Masterson Station Park for its soccer fields, cross-country meets, or as the site of the Lyon's Bluegrass Fair. But few know that this 660-acre park was part of a larger tract of land once owned by Richard Masterson, one of the early settlers of Lexington, who on this site built one of the first two-story log houses in Kentucky. The first Methodist church in the state was also built here.

In the 1920s, the US government purchased the land to establish one of two federal narcotic farms "for the confinement and treatment of persons addicted to the use of habit-forming narcotic drugs" (Public Law 70-672). Addicts were "voluntarily" committed for what became mostly experimental treatments, including the use of methadone for heroin users. Other research included the study of acute versus prolonged drug withdrawal. Patients were assigned various chores on the "farm" as part of their therapy, including working in the fields and the milking parlor, and raising hogs.

In the early 1970s, the federal government turned part of the property over to Lexington (Fayette County) for use as a public park. The government retained the rest of the property for more confining purposes. The western boundary of the park is currently the women's Federal Prison and Medical Center, which briefly housed "Squeaky" Fromme (one-time member of the Charles Manson family) and billionaire real-estate heiress Leona Helmsley. The northern boundary of the park is the minimum-security Blackburn Correctional Complex for men.

The barns and milking parlors of the Narcotics Farm were converted by the city for equestrian use; the plowed fields to soccer pitches; and open space for use by the model airplane and in-line hockey clubs. A dog park has also been added... woof!

Casual hikers, mountain bikers, and runners can travel along a 4-mile grass path that runs the perimeter of the park and a 0.5 mile paved shared-use connector trail to Masterson Station Drive.

After turning into the park, the paved connector trail can be seen crossing the main road. Parking can usually be found on the right, alongside the road. Once you have a feel for the lay of the land, the perimeter trail can be accessed at many other places and parking lots, but this is a good starting point.

Take the paved sidewalk to your right until you are at the eastern park boundary adjacent to the Masterson Station subdivision. Turn left up the grass path that follows the perimeter of the park. This will begin a counterclockwise rotation on the trail. Continue walking, keeping the park on your left and the houses on your right. At the back of the park the trail takes a sharp left turn and runs adjacent to a small creek. You are now on the northern end of the park. In the springtime you'll be greeted with a beautiful redbud display, while the native cane greens with the summer season. Cross over a small gravel road and continue with the creek on your right.

After crossing the main paved road, the trail climbs a small hill on your left, alongside a line of mature trees. Near the large pines you'll step over a small concrete marker that begins the 5K races. Take a sharp right and walk down another small hill, over the creek, and up towards the milking parlor and silos. The trail then takes a another sharp left and follows the chain link fence boundary with the Federal Prison. Stay on your side of the prison fence, don't make any sudden moves, or take any video. Smile for the camera.

The trail eventually joins the creek again, with beautiful views of open fields and horse jumps. Most of the trees in the low-lying areas at Masterson are a direct result of Reforest the Bluegrass efforts. The trail continues to follow the western boundary of the park before turning left once again (roughly parallel to Leestown Road.) You should see your vehicle any time.

Other good parking places include the small lot on the top of the hill (in the middle of the park) and the large lot at the rear of the park (near the barns). The perimeter trail can be easily accessed from each of these lots.

As you finish your walk, listen to the birds sing and feel the sweet breeze upon your face, and remind yourself how good it feels to be free.

Side Trip:
Other parks in urban Lexington offer unpaved trails including Gleneagles Greenway (0.7 miles, off of Polo Blvd featuring native plantings); Cross Keys Park (0.3 miles, off Cross Keys Road); and Stonewall Park (0.3 miles, off Cornwall Drive). Also see the entries for Veteran's Park and The Arboretum.

Masterson Station Park
3051 Leestown Road
Lexington, KY 40511
Web: lexingtonky.gov/index.aspx?page=2101

34 Maywoods

A nice hike through quiet deciduous woods, over creeks, and up and down knobs.

Trail Length: Up to 6.0 miles

Facilities: No bathrooms. Drinking water available seasonally. Picnic shelter.

Hours: Tuesday through Sunday; 8 am-5 pm. Closed Mondays.

Additional Information: A small lake is open to the public for largemouth bass and bluegill fishing. Pets are not permitted on the property.

Directions: Drive south on I-75. Take Berea exit #76. Turn right (west) on KY 21. Drive 2.4 miles. Turn left on KY 954 (Cartersville Road). Drive 5 miles. Turn left on KY 3246 (Fall Lick Road). Drive 5.2 miles. Turn left on Maywoods Road. Follow this gravel road through the gate, past the lake, and up to the lodge. Park there.

Public and private universities are occasionally bequeathed or directly purchase property in order to protect rare species, conduct research activities, or provide environmental education opportunities for students. Eastern Kentucky University is fortunate to have the 1,700-acre tract of land known as Maywoods. This natural area and wildlife refuge straddles the Garrard-Rockcastle county lines, located in the Knobs Region west of Berea.

With the exception of Tuesday and Thursday mornings during the school year, which are frequently devoted to student groups, there's a good chance you'll have the trails to yourself. There is some limited parking near the lake; otherwise park near the lodge to access most trails.

If you're looking for something short, try the Lake Side Path, which runs behind the lodge; the Oak Hickory Trail, which leaves from the opposite side of the parking lot; or the Lake Trail, which is accessed from the other side of the earthen berm, which impounds Lake Edminston. Each of these trails is less than a third of a mile in length.

For something longer, the 1.5-mile Forest Ecosystem Trail loop offers detailed signage describing, well, the forest ecosystem you pass through. This is a great trail for younger kids with lots of energy and short attention spans.

If you're looking for more of a workout, piece together several of the trails to form a good 6-mile loop. Start by picking up the Oak Hickory Trail from the backside of the parking lot. In about 0.15 miles, or about ten minutes of walking, you'll meet up with the Forest Ecosystem Trail. Turn right and follow this trail up and down the sides of several knobs and across multiple creeks. Be on the lookout for some magnificent geodes scattered along the creek beds, being sure to leave them for subsequent hikers to admire.

In about a mile, the Ridgerunner Trail joins the Forest Ecosystem Trail. Bear left (east) on the Ridgerunner for a 4-mile loop that will test your endurance for some real knob climbing. Hiking poles come in handy on sections of this trail, as the short but steep ascents and descents can leave you a bit winded. After the first mile, the Ridgerunner is not particularly well-maintained, but the trail is extremely well-marked with orange blazes and other signage.

A word of caution about the Ridgerunner Trail: During the summer months you may find yourself hiking mid-calf through poison ivy, smilax, and other weeds. Long pants, firmly cuffed at the ankles, along with some insect repellent may work wonders to keep the ticks at bay. Rue the day to discover you've walked through a nest of seed ticks! For this reason, you may want to save the Ridgerunner Trail for an early spring hike, to enjoy the bounty of wildflowers that call this place home. Alternately, the glorious colors of autumn abound at Maywoods. Given how well-marked the trails are, winter hiking is also a great option.

The Ridgerunner Trail rejoins the Forest Ecosystem Trail just a few yards from where you left the latter. Continue your clockwise hike by heading north towards Lake Edminston. The one-third mile Lake Trail loop is worth the time. Despite some misleading signage here, you must walk across the earthen berm, which impounds the lake, and follow the gravel road back to the lodge.

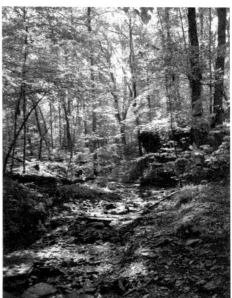

Trail Map: http://goo.gl/MyCI7g

Side Trip:
EKU also owns the 60-acre Taylor Fork Ecological Area, located south of their main campus in Richmond, KY. There is a short interpretive trail that passes through mostly open fields. http://naturalareas.eku.edu/taylor-fork-ecological-area

Maywoods Environmental and Educational Laboratory
447 Maywoods Drive
Crab Orchard, KY 40419
Phone: (859) 925-2274
Web: http://naturalareas.eku.edu/maywoods-environmental-and-educational-laboratory

35 McConnell Springs

A small urban park and nature center, interlaced with walking trails, historical sites, and disappearing creeks.

Trail Length: 0.25 to 2 miles

Facilities: Education (nature) Center, bathrooms, drinking water.

Hours: The park is open daily year-round, dawn to dusk. The Education Center is open Monday–Saturday, 9 am-5 pm; Sunday 1-5 pm.

Directions: Head out of downtown Lexington on Old Frankfort Pike (Manchester Street). Just past Forbes Road, take a left on McConnell Springs Drive, a left on Cahill Drive, and a right on Rebmann Lane.

For a taste of history and a smidgen of the outdoors, McConnell Springs may be just the ticket for the urban outdoorsmen. Their website describes it best: *"A passive recreational park."* Back in 1775, when Kentucky County was but a wild appendage of the state of Virginia, William McConnell camped at these springs with some of his buddies, several of who became the founding fathers of Lexington. The area later served as the location for a gristmill, gunpowder factory, and a dairy farm. Now a National Registered Historic Site, the park also serves as a bookend for the fledgling "distillery district" of west Lexington.

The park itself consists of a nature center housed in an organically-shaped modern stone structure, walking trails, and well-executed signage describing the springs, limestone bedrock, wetlands, and sinks. McConnell Springs can be a wonderful walking woods for children and the mobility-challenged with its paved trails, well-constructed walkways, and interesting sights. It also contains perhaps Lexington's first "bridge to nowhere" as part of an admirable attempt to improve the quality of the water flowing through its boundaries and beyond, and to reduce the park's overly abundant mosquito population. The pavilion and nature center can also be rented out for private parties in the off-hours.

McConnell Springs is most enjoyable during the non-peak season (primarily days of the week and throughout the winter) and during special events it holds on a regular basis, including Barrel Tasting for the Springs; Founder's Day and Colonial Crafts Festival; and their "work-out weekend" where volunteers have the chance to get their hands around the necks of some unwanted invasive species.

Side Trip:

Driving (or better yet, cycling) back to downtown Lexington, try and follow Town Branch Creek as it winds along Manchester Street, only to disappear at Rupp Arena. See if you can identify the Old Woolen Mill (circa 1820), the James McConnell dry-laid stone house (circa 1790), and the James E. Pepper Distillery (the birthplace of "Old 1776").

The up-and-coming Distillery District along Manchester Street has an amazing and growing selection of restaurants, breweries, art galleries, and more.

McConnell Springs
416 Rebmann Lane
Lexington, KY 40504
Phone: (859) 225-4073
mcconnellsprings.org

36 Natural Arch Scenic Area

A short walk to one of the largest arches in the state.

Trail Length: 5 minutes or 6.7 miles

Facilities: Picnic tables and shelters, drinking water, and toilets.

Hours: 6 am-10 pm

Additional Information: There is a $3 daily use fee, payable on-site. If you have an annual Daniel Boone National Forest Pass you may use it here. Pets are permitted.

Directions: Drive south on I-75. Take exit #62 (US 25) south towards KY 461. Follow KY 461 for 18 miles. Bear right (west) on KY 80 for 6 miles. Take a left on KY 914 W for 4.5 miles and another left on KY 1247 S for 4 miles. Merge onto US 27 S, towards Whitley City. Follow US 27 south for 15 miles. Turn right (west) on KY 927, Day Ridge Road. Travel 2 miles. The park is on your right. Park in the lot at the top of the hill or on your right, closer to the amphitheater. There is a nice view of the arch from the upper lot.

Hmm.....what is the largest natural arch in Kentucky? Just what measurement are we talking about here? Height? Width? Diagonal span? And how do you measure an arch? Triangulation? Photo estimation? Differential GPS? And what's the difference between a natural arch and a natural bridge? If these are the kinds of questions that keep you up at night, check out the web site of the non-profit Natural Arch and Bridge Society. It makes for great cocktail talk and you'll be the hit of the party.

Established in 1961, the Scenic Area protects 945 acres of land that admirably served as home to many prehistoric peoples and as the former hunting grounds of the Cherokee. With a span of 100 feet, Natural Arch is ranked fourth largest in the state, and is clearly smaller than Mantle Rock, which has a span of 188 feet (located outside of Livingston, KY). But Mantle Rock is only 30 foot high. More trivia!

After paying your fee, park in either lot and follow the signs and paved trail past the amphitheater and on to the stone terrace and scenic overlook. The good thing is that you only have to walk about 5 minutes before your first view of the arch. Consequently, you leave lots of tourists happy with their achievement and you're left with most of the trails to yourself. By seeing the arch first you can really enjoy the rest of the hike, without spending all day waiting for the punch line. From the overlook, continue along the paved trail and down several short flights of stone steps. Ignore the small unmarked trail that enters on your left——this is where you will come out on the Buffalo Canyon Trail. Continue walking towards the arch.

When viewed from the overlook, Natural Arch looks big, but not that big. It's not until you walk under the arch that you really appreciate the immensity of what Mother Nature has created. If you look closely, you can spot several other smaller arches. After passing under the arch, you are immediately overshadowed by a tremendous rockhouse, randomly painted across its base with beautifully-colored, dayglow-green lichen.

Just past the rockhouse, bear left on the unmarked, half-mile Natural Loop Arch Trail #510. Take your time as you wind counterclockwise around the sandstone-

glomerate bluffs pocked with quartz pebbles. There are some really cool rock formations along this trail, so take it slow. The park map says this loop is a mile, but that counts walking from the parking lot and back again.

After hiking the loop, pass back under the arch a second time to pick up the 5-mile Buffalo Canyon Trail #508. Follow the wood walkway under the rockhouse again, but instead of bearing left on the loop trail, continue hiking straight on the Buffalo Canyon Trail, also unmarked. This sounds confusing, but just keep an eye on the map.

The Buffalo Canyon Trail begins its descent along Spruce Creek and a newly-erected bridge that must have been built with handrails for Kobe Bryant. This area is a good place for wildflower hunting. In a little over a mile, the Buffalo Canyon Trail joins a gravel road heading north, where you'll pass a most unusual collection of cabins, lean-tos, and water storage tanks. Quite honestly, you're not sure if you've reached an abandoned snake-handling school, a church's summer retreat center, or simply a family compound frozen in time. Don't tempt fate: Stay right at the intersection with Young Farm Road and continue along the gravel road.

Just after the road traverses a low-water crossing, bear left (west) on an old logging road, as the gravel road bears right (east). Follow the logging road along Cooper Creek for roughly another mile, until the trail takes a sharp left turn and heads south. Here you will be forced to cross Cooper Creek, which at high water can be quite challenging. The trail itself crosses a deep pool, so you may have more luck crossing just upstream where the water is shallower or risk walking (aka bum-scooting) across an old log that bridges the watery divide.

At this point the trail begins a gradual ascent along Cutoff Branch creek. If you're lucky enough to be hiking on a sunny day, the light sparkling through the hemlock needles is enough to put the glitter of My Little Pony to shame. In another mile or so, you will pass an interesting rockhouse that could also be considered an arch of sorts. Take some time to explore the area. You'll be very close to Big Cutoff, a narrow gap between two imposing ridges. A final mile of hiking will bring you back to Natural Arch Trail. Turn right (south) to return to the trailhead and parking lot.

Trail Map: http://goo.gl/uCXs7X

Side Trip:
If you're up for a little more hiking or simply a drive-by scenic view, leave the park and turn right on Day Ridge Road (KY 927). In just a short distance you'll see a small parking area on your right and the trailhead for the out-and-back, 1-mile Panoramic View Trail. While you can't see the arch from here, there are several nice views. Drive just a little bit further down the road and there are pull-offs on both sides of the road, with more good views, particularly in the fall.

Stearns Ranger District
3320 Hwy. 27 North
Whitley City, KY 42653
Phone: (606) 376-5323
Website: http://goo.gl/w8GmK5

Natural Bridge State Park

Originally mined for saltpeter to make gunpowder during the War of 1812, the area surrounding Natural Bridge was established as a public park in 1896 by the Lexington and Eastern Railroad Company. Accessible only by train, the park was later given to the state of Kentucky in 1926 as a gift from the Louisville Nashville Railroad, which hauled coal and lumber out of the region. Encompassing 2500 acres, including 1200 acres classified as a nature preserve, the park has 22 miles of backcountry hiking trails.

For many tourists, Natural Bridge serves as their first entrée to the natural sandstone arches that are prevalent across eastern Kentucky. A combination of weathering (cycles of freezing and thawing) and erosion (both water and wind) has carved the rock into delightful land-based bridges. Both Natural Bridge State Park and the adjacent Red River Gorge Geological Area are located within the Daniel Boone National Forest, and share a lot of the same geological formations. While Natural Bridge State Park has a handful of these arches, Red River Gorge has over one hundred natural arches, and the Big South Fork Recreational Area (straddling the KY-TN border) has hundreds more.

In 1927 the state of Kentucky built a three-story log hotel for their guests. Unfortunately the hotel burned in the early 1960s and was replaced in 1962 with a stone and wood structure. Although backcountry camping is not permitted, there are two established campgrounds in the park. Other amenities include a swimming pool, paddleboats, restaurant, picnic shelters, and playgrounds.

Several of the trails in Natural Bridge State Park, with proper oversight, can be suitable for children. Although most of the trails include some (if not many) steps, children have a much faster recovery time than adults do. However, some kids do not have the stamina of adults——or the fear of heights. Watch them carefully, if not hold their hands, the entire time they are near the cliffs or other dangerous parts of these trails.

As much as we hate to discourage winter hiking, this area might not be the best choice for below freezing temperatures. Ice and snow could make any and all of these trails extremely treacherous.

Also note the frequent signs guaranteeing a $500 fine for "carving." And we're not talking turkey. Remember the adage "Fools' names and fools' faces are often seen in public places." You'll have to profess your love somewhere else.

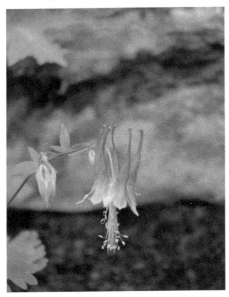

We present two different options for hiking the area surrounding Natural Bridge: the Laurel Ridge Trail Loop and the Rock Garden Trail Loop (both about 3.5 miles long.) A longer loop option is available by combining the Sand Gap Arch Trail and Hood's Branch Trail, for a total of about 12.5 miles. These last two trails are rated moderate to strenuous and may be a bit much for many of our readers.

Natural Bridge State Park
2135 Natural Bridge Road
Slade, KY 40376-9701
Phone: (606) 663-2214
**Web: parks.ky.gov/findparks/
resortparks/nb**

37 Laurel Ridge Trail Loop

Spectacular views from above and below Natural Bridge arch.

Trail Length: 3.5 miles
Facilities: Bathrooms and more, but be sure to bring water on the trail.
Hours: Hikers must be out by sunset.
Additional Information: Trail maps are available at the Hemlock Lodge. No pets allowed, on or off leash.
Directions: Drive east on I-64. Just past Winchester, take exit #98 for the Bert T. Combs Mountain Parkway. Stay on the Parkway until Slade, exit #33. Turn right on KY 11. Drive 2.4 miles (past both the Lodge and the picnic entrances.) Turn right into the large lot indicated as trail parking for Natural Bridge.

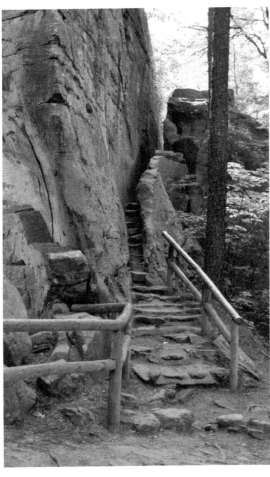

The Laurel Ridge Trail Loop combines four shorter trails to get the hiker up and over the arch and back down again—hopefully in one piece. As the sign says: *Visitors must be prepared to meet and accept nature on its own terms.* Although an easy hike for some, this trail combination involves several sets of stairs, short (but steep) elevation changes, and exposed cliff tops.

Begin at the parking lot described above. This trail sequence begins at the far end of the lot, on the 0.25-mile Lakeside Trail. Descend the set of stairs and walk along the large pond formed by damming the Middle Fork of the Red River. The trail continues on a gravel path that leads to a bridge and what they call Hoedown Island (named for the square dances held here). Take a quick look at the gift shop, top off a water bottle, and take advantage of the flush toilets while you can.

To the left of the gift shop you'll see a kiosk with a posted trail map. Head uphill to what is called the "Original Trail". This is the main path to Natural Bridge arch. Only 0.75 miles in length, the trail climbs steadily. Multiple benches and small covered shelters are closer by to provide a much-appreciated respite for many walkers. Once at the base of Natural Bridge, be sure to soak in the beauty and marvel at Mother Nature's artwork.

From underneath the arch, you will see a very narrow set of stone steps leading up to the top of the sandstone arch. The view at the top is worth the climb. Natural Bridge is estimated to be 78' long and 65' high. If you do the math, a fall from the top of the arch would be a 65' drop. A large shaded pavilion is also on top for those wanting to rest and enjoy the sights.

Continue walking to the opposite (north) end of the arch. From here you can pick up the 0.75-mile Laurel Ridge Trail, which takes you past the Skylift to Lookout Point and Lover's Leap, both with scenic views to the east. The ridge is loaded with mountain laurel (blooming in May) and wild blueberries (which ripen midsummer).

To return, backtrack a short distance along Laurel Ridge Trail until you get to either Needle's Eye Stairway or Devil's Gulch. Both of these short connector trails are extremely steep descents to the base of the ridge and converge with Battleship Rock Trail (BRT), which runs along the base of the ridge that forms Natural Bridge. Take a right on BRT (heading south) for about a half-mile until you rejoin the Original Trail. To return to the parking lot, retrace your steps back down the Original Trail to the Lakeside Trail and your vehicle.

Side Trips:

Leaving the parking lot, turn left on KY 11. Turn right first chance you get, at the sign to Whittleton Campground (Forest Road #216). At the end of the campground loop is a short trail (one-third of a mile) that leads to Henson's Cave Arch. At the far end of Whittleton Branch Road is a 2-mile trail (round-trip) to Whittleton Arch.

Another way cool side trip would be the Kentucky Reptile Zoo. The serpentarium is located off KY 11 between the Mountain Parkway and Natural Bridge State Park. They do live venom extractions ("milkings" used for pharmaceutical research and the production of antiserum) at 1 pm daily. For more information visit kyreptilezoo.org or call (606) 663-9160. Their address is 200 L&E Railroad, Slade, KY 40376.

38 Rock Garden Trail Loop

A quiet trail studded with spring wildflowers, huge boulders, and the famous 'Balanced Rock.'

Trail Length: 3.25 miles
Facilities: Bathrooms and more, but be sure to bring water on the trail.
Hours: Hikers must be out by sunset.
Additional Information: Trail maps are available at the Hemlock Lodge. This area can be quite crowded during the summer, and during pretty spring and fall weekends. No pets allowed.

Directions: Drive east on I-64. Just past Winchester, take exit #98 for the Bert T. Combs Mountain Parkway. Stay on the Parkway until Slade, exit #33. Turn right on KY 11. Drive 2.4 miles (past both the Lodge and the picnic entrances). Turn right into the large lot indicated as trail parking for Natural Bridge.

This loop leaves from the same location as the other Natural Bridge trails, but avoids more of the crowds seeking the views from atop the arch. You may want to read the Laurel Ridge Trail Loop description if you are wanting views from atop Natural Bridge Arch.

Begin at the parking lot described above. Follow the directions for the Laurel Ridge Trail Loop until you come to a sign for the "Original Trail." Follow the

Original Trail up a short distance until you see Battleship Rock Trail on your right. Take this trail yet another short distance until you join with Rock Garden Trail. Eureka!

The Rock Garden Trail circles counterclockwise around the base of Natural Bridge arch. The first half of this 1.75-mile trail is rich with wildflowers in the spring including Solomon's seal, mayapple, trillium, rock cress, hepatica, ferns, and wild yam. Wild turkeys are known to haunt this hillside and even raise their young here. The back side of Rock Garden Trail hugs the western side of the ridge that forms Natural Bridge. Here the sandstone surface is stunning with incredible swirling patterns and pockmarks, providing luscious eye candy for all who hike this trail.

Rock Garden Trail ends below Natural Bridge arch. Take the stairs to the top of the arch, turn right, and join Balanced Rock Trail (you will also see signs for Sand Gap Trail.) This 0.75-mile trail will take you down from the ridge to a rock formation that involves, well, a huge balancing rock that really is quite magnificent. A little further you'll pass a large rockhouse and cave opening just before you rejoin the Original Trail. To return to your vehicle, retrace your steps back to the Lakeside Trail.

Side Trip:
Leaving the parking lot, turn left on KY 11. Just past the main park entrance, you'll see a sign on your right for Miguel's Pizza (and Rock Climbing Shop). Incredible hand-made pizza, organic toppings, Ale-8-One, free wi-fi, breakfast burritos, $2 per night camping...Need we say more? All Miguel asks is that you keep your dogs on a leash——the chickens like it better that way. 1890 Natural Bridge Road. Slade, KY 40376. (606) 663-1975.

39 Perryville Battlefield State Historic Site

Lots of mowed paths through open fields, punctuated with historical markers.

Trail Length: 1 to 10.5 miles

Facilities: Restrooms, picnic tables and shelters, playground, and a museum.

Hours: Grounds are open sunrise to sunset, year-round.

Additional Information: The museum and gift shop is open Monday–Saturday, 9 am–5 pm; Sunday 11 am-5 pm. Closes November 27th. December through March, open by appointment only. The museum has a $4 entrance fee ($2.50 for children 12 and under), but access to the park is free.

Directions: Drive south on Nicholasville Road (US 27 S). From Man O' War and Nicholasville Road, drive 22.8 miles; turn right on KY 34 W towards Danville. Drive another 6.7 miles; turn left on Wilderness Road. In 0.3 mile, take a right on Main Street. Main merges with KY 52 W. Stay on KY 52 for 10.4 miles. In the small town of Perryville, turn right on Jackson Street (KY 1920). Travel another 2.2 miles before taking your final left into the Perryville Battlefield State Historic Site.

With almost 750 acres and 10.5 miles of interpretive hiking trails, this park has a lot of place to roam. The Kentucky Department of Parks has worked quite diligently to maintain the site as it looked in 1862 when the Battle of Perryville was fought. Widely considered a crucial battle for both sides in the Civil War, the Confederate army won the battle but retreated back to Tennessee as fresh Union troops were advancing. Over 7,500 men on both sides were either killed or wounded in the battle.

Today, the park is crisscrossed with mowed paths and historical markers commemorating the battle. A free walking trail guide is available at the museum and includes more than 37 stops. The "short-loop" includes stops 1-12 and covers 1.3 miles. The "long-loop" adds sites 16-19 and covers 3 miles. In total, there are 28 markers and an additional nine historical sites identified in the park. Although water and bathrooms are available at the museum, you are advised to be prepared before starting out on the trails. A good hat and ample sunscreen are also suggested.

Trail maps: http://goo.gl/4FJRrd

Side Trip:
After leaving the park and returning to Perryville, turn down Buell Street, named after Major General Don Carlos Buell (from Ohio) who led the Union forces. The street hosts a small number of shops that look like they were built back when hardtack was still soft. Bragg Street, named after General Braxton Bragg of the Confederate forces, is one block over, on the other side of the creek.

Perryville Battlefield State Historic Site
825 Battlefield Road
Perryville, KY 40468
Phone: (859) 332-8631
**Web: http://parks.ky.gov/parks/historicsites/
perryville-battlefield/**

40 Pilot Knob State Nature Preserve

Pull on your felt hat and stand where Daniel Boone once did, gazing softly at spectacular views of central Kentucky, the Knobs, and the Cumberland Plateau.

Trail Length: 0.8 to 5.1 miles
Facilities: None
Hours: Daily, sunrise to sunset
Additional Information: Don't take the little kids on this one. Although, no one would ever hear them scream…
Directions: Follow I-64 east out of Lexington. On the other side of Winchester, bear right on the Bert T. Combs Mountain Parkway. Take exit #16, toward KY 82 and Clay City / Irvine. Turn right on KY 15 N, traveling another 2.9 miles. Take another right on Brush Creek Road for 1.5 miles, until it dead-ends in a wide gravel circle.

Covering a large portion of the 742-acre preserve, the main trail goes up. And down. And up. And down. If you're in good shape, we would rate it moderate. Otherwise, it's rated strenuous. Nonetheless, if your goal is to hike the Continental Divide next summer, strap on a 35-pound pack and power walk this one.

There's a good chance you'll have this Preserve to yourself. Much of Pilot Knob is second growth forest, populated with oak (including blackjack oak), hickory, and pine. The abundance of acorns provides a continuous food source for the deer and other small mammals of the area. The birds are plentiful here, brightly chattering about the day, while the constant clucking of wild turkeys may have you writing rap

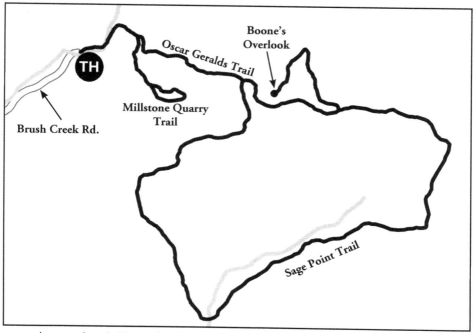

songs in your head. From the riot of wildflowers in the spring to the panorama of fall colors, Pilot Knob is a four-season getaway.

After parking, follow the old road a short distance, cross the creek, and go up the steps past the steel gate. Another 50 yards and you'll find the information kiosk with a large posted map (none available for pick-up) and a visitor's sign-in sheet.

A short distance from the kiosk you'll see the Millstone Quarry Trail on your right, which is about a mile in length (despite what the posted map says). A bit hard to follow in places, the trail is flagged with red, pink, and orange plastic ties around some of the trees. The path will lead you to an area where conglomerate rock (a type of sandstone, comprised of sand and quartz) was made into millstones. A few works-in-progress remain and we bet you can't lift one.

Heading further up the main path, the Oscar Geralds, Jr. Trail takes you to a rock bluff known as Boone's Overlook. The trail begins with a strong vertical ascent and doesn't let up. Halfway to the top you'll see the Sage Point Trail come in on your right. Bear left and continue climbing. The Sage Point Trail will intersect again on your right. Bear left once more. From the trailhead to the top of the rock bluff is 1.25 miles, one way.

Boone's Overlook provides beautiful views of the Bluegrass Region to the northwest, and the Knobs and Cumberland Plateau to the south. It's a great place for lunch, or just sitting with a good book in hand. We can easily imagine Daniel enjoying the peace and solitude found here. Boone supposedly claimed all he needed was "a good gun, a good horse, and a good wife." Any woman left with ten children while her husband gallivanted around the wilderness deserves her own place in history.

On your way back down from Boone's Overlook, take a left on Sage Point Trail to add another 2 miles to your day. A loop trail, Sage Point follows a narrow spine down to a well-maintained gravel road. Take a right and walk the road for a short distance until you see the trail marker on your right indicating the path back into the woods. (If you take a left and walk up this road to the Preserve boundary line and back down again you will add an additional mile to your hike.) Both Geralds and Sage Point trails are blazed in red and the Preserve boundary is blazed with bright yellow signs and parallel orange stripes painted around some of the trees.

Once the Sage Point Trail enters the woods again, a gentle descent brings you across a creek and under some power lines. Early summer hikers will be met with the sweet smell of wild roses, while mid-summer visitors will have the opportunity to munch on a few wild blackberries. Across another creek, the trail climbs once more, before meeting up with the Oscar Geralds Trail again. A left turn, coupled with a strong descent, will bring you back to the kiosk.

Side Trip:

If you have any daylight left, you may want to explore Hidden Valley Wildlife Management Area (WMA). As you leave Brush Creek Road, turn left on KY 15 and take an immediate right on Hidden Valley Road. Although no formal trails have been developed, the 542-acre tract is accessible by paved, gravel, and dirt roads.

Pilot Knob State Nature Preserve
Brush Creek Road
Clay City, KY 40312
Web: naturepreserves.ky.gov/naturepreserves/Pages/pilotknob.aspx

41 Quiet Trails State Nature Preserve

Snug against the bend of the Licking River, the name says it all.

Trail Length: 3.1 miles

Facilities: None

Hours: Daily, sunrise to sunset

Additional Information: No facilities. You may want to print out the map from the website before you go. No pets, leashed or not.

Directions: From the intersection of I-75/64 and North Broadway, drive north on Paris Pike (US 27/68). Stay on US 27 all the way to Cynthiana. Eleven miles north of town, turn right onto KY 1284, which leads to the small hamlet of Sunrise. At the four-way stop, continue straight, which is Pugh's Ferry Road. At the next fork, bear LEFT (Moore's Mill Road goes to the right). The parking lot for the Preserve is 1.8 miles from Sunrise.

Bill and Martha Wiglesworth, who had the intent of creating their own nature sanctuary, originally purchased most of this land. The couple worked to reestablish native species of wildflowers and grasses, plant trees, and provide for wildlife. In 1991, they donated the property to the Kentucky State Nature Preserves Commission. Their personal touches are evident.

The lack of road noise makes this one of the quietest hiking areas in central Kentucky. With 165 acres, the Preserve trails start hilltop before tumbling down creekside on the Deep Hollow Trail. Be sure to follow the Challenger and River's Edge trails for views of the Licking River.

A small wildlife-viewing hut is located on the property, although given its infrequent use, the wildlife appear to have taken up residence inside the hut itself.

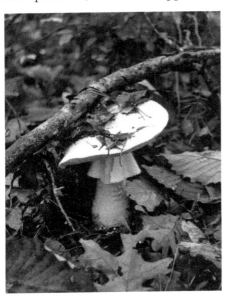

One visitor found a black widow in the sign-in box and another noted that a feral cat had made good use of the old outhouse. But for some of us, these are all signs that there is a good chance that we will have the trails to ourselves and might actually get to see some live critters. The abundance of wildlife, including pileated woodpeckers and wild turkey, make this a rich walk in the woods.

Quiet Trails State Nature Preserve
Pugh's Ferry Road
Sunrise, KY 41004
Web: naturepreserves.ky.gov/
naturepreserves/
Pages/quiettrails.aspx

42 Raven Run Nature Sanctuary

Raven Run is known for its spring wildflowers, multitude of small waterfalls, and vibrant fall colors.

Trail Length: 2 to 10 miles

Facilities: Nature center, restrooms, and drinking water are available.

Hours: Daily 9 am–5 pm (trails close at 4:30 pm). Closed Thanksgiving Day and during the Christmas holiday (Dec. 24-26).

Additional Information: To protect this heavily used Nature Sanctuary, please do not hike off-trail, or wade or hike in any of the creeks.

Directions: Take Richmond Road east (out of Lexington) and turn right on Old Richmond Road (US 25), directly across from the entrance to Jacobson Park. Go approximately 3.4 miles to Jack's Creek Pike (KY 1975). Turn right at the country store. Go about 5.2 miles. Shortly after a split log fence, followed with a chain link fence, you will see the park entrance on your left.

Alternative route from south Lexington: Head south on Tates Creek Road. From Man O' War Boulevard, travel approximately 7.8 miles. Take a sharp left on Spears Road, near a small cluster of buildings. Travel 1.6 miles on Spears Road. Turn right on Jacks Creek Pike (KY 1975). Drive about a mile. Shortly after a split log fence, followed with a chain link fence, you will see the park entrance on your left.

Raven Run Nature Sanctuary is the first, and perhaps the only, park in Fayette County with more trees than grass, and more trails (at least seven) than ball fields (zero). People actually go there to hike. With over 734 acres, the terrain at Raven Run varies from rolling meadows to eastern hardwoods, complemented with creeks, waterfalls, and an overlook featuring the Kentucky River palisades.

The sanctuary is a wonderful, 4-season woodland getaway. Spectacular spring wildflowers, beautiful summer meadows, brilliant fall foliage, and snowy winter scenery can all be found at Raven Run.

One of the best times to hike the park is during the winter months when crowds are significantly reduced and the abundance of wildlife is evident, including wild turkey and deer. After a fresh snow, animal tracks provide an interesting diversion to the leafless landscape. Hiking at Raven Run is also a good time to bring a flower or tree identification book, or an animal track guide.

At the far end of the parking lot, behind the small stone building, follow the sidewalk across the paved road, and walk another 75 yards to the staffed nature center. It is kid-friendly and has many hands-on displays, including aquariums, animal pelts, and skeletal remains to pique the interest of the whole family. Trail maps, restrooms, and potable water are available. Be sure to sign in.

Raven Run Nature Sanctuary conducts several special programs throughout the year. A visit to the park's website includes a description of the various programs and an events calendar. Typical planned activities include an archeological excavation of the Prather house; a Halloween program for the kids; birding; wildflower identification; night insect walks; and star gazing.

The trails start behind the nature center. After picking up a map, you'll see that the 4-mile red trail basically encircles the perimeter of the park and is comprised mostly of a lightly wooded, rocky terrain. This moderate loop trail is a good introduction to the sanctuary and many of the park's highlights can be reached via spurs off the red trail, including the ever-popular overlook at the Kentucky River.

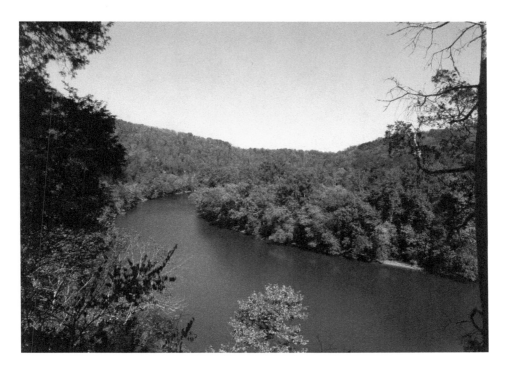

The green trail has multiple arteries that connect various points of the red trail and is comprised mostly of open meadows. The orange trail, a detour off the red trail, also is a meadow trail and summer hikes hold promise of both yellow and purple coneflowers. The blue trails serve as connectors between other trails.

The white trail is a worthwhile appendage to the red trail that takes the hiker to the fork of two creeks and the site of an old gristmill. Similarly, the short, but steep yellow trail takes you creek side, into what they call the Flower Bowl preserve. Raven Run has over 350 varieties of wildflowers, and the spring season showcases their glory, including blue-eyed Marys, yellow trout lilies, and Dutchman's britches.

The one-mile Freedom Trail is paved and designed for the visually-impaired. Strollers are also welcome, but be sure the brakes are in good wokring order.

This is a high-use natural area, and solitude may be hard to find. With so many visitors, some trails are "loved to death," causing many trails to be extremely muddy after even a light rain. We need more parks and nature preserves!

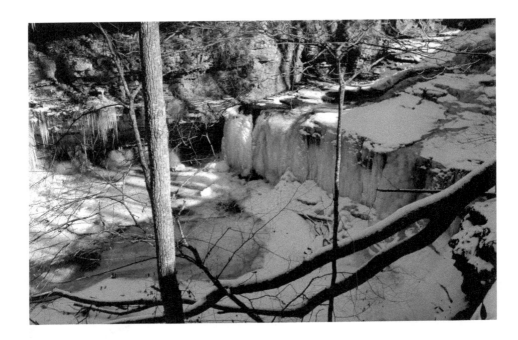

Side Trip:
The Valley View Ferry operates on the Kentucky River at the end of Tates Creek Road (KY 169). Since 1785, this ferry (well, not the same exact boat) has carted people and their belongings between Fayette, Madison, and Jessamine counties. The charter for the ferry was signed by Virginia Governor Patrick Henry.

The free ferry (at the time of this writing) is occasionally closed due to high water. Hours of operation are Monday–Friday, 6 am-6 pm; and Saturday–Sunday, 8 am-8 pm. Open daily except Christmas Day. The status of the ferry can be found by calling (859) 258-3611.

Raven Run Nature Sanctuary
5888 Jacks Creek Pike
Lexington, KY 40515
Phone: (859) 272-6105
Web: lexingtonky.gov/index.aspx?page=276

Red River Gorge

The Red River Geological Area is part of the Cumberland (or Pottsville) Escarpment at the edge of the Cumberland Plateau. Located within the Daniel Boone National Forest, the 26,000 acre "Gorge" (as locals affectionately refer to it) has been sanctioned as a National Natural Landmark, and the Red River as a National Wild and Scenic River. These designations effectively ended thirty years of misguided efforts to dam the river for downstream flood control.

Richly endowed with natural stone arches, rockhouses, scenic waterfalls, and towering sandstone cliffs, the Gorge offers three basic kinds of hiking trails— creekside paths through majestic hemlock groves and rhododendron thickets; ridgetop trails with panoramic views; and destination arches. Many of these vistas are found just a short distance from a paved road or parking area, while longer trails are available for the ardent backpacker.

Red River Gorge is also a renowned rock climber's paradise. Famous for both its traditional and sport climbing routes, the Gorge attracts climbers from all over the world and has almost a cult following.

Unfortunately the Gorge has also been a popular party spot and numerous deaths have occurred as the result of late night forays. Cliffs, alcohol, and drugs just don't mix. So only use water in your bottle and tread safely.

With over 100 natural arches, the Red River Gorge is a delight for hikers of all shapes and sizes. With many trails only an hour away from Lexington, it's easy to see why it's such a popular day hiking destination. We've provided three sample hikes just to whet your appetite. We know you'll be back for more.

USDA Forest Service: Daniel Boone National Forest
1700 Bypass Road
Winchester, KY 40391
Phone: (859) 745-3100
Web: fs.fed.us/r8/boone/districts/cumberland/
redriver_gorge.shtml

Some excellent maps can be found at **redrivergorge.com.**

43 Auxier Ridge/Courthouse Rock Trail Loop

A ridgetop trail with panoramic views of Courthouse Rock and Double Arch, before traveling through hemlock forests and fern-infused hillsides.

Trail Length: 5.2 miles

Facilities: Pit toilets and picnic tables at trailhead. No drinking water available.

Hours: Be off the trail by dark.

Additional Information: Overnight backpackers must obtain a permit.

Directions: Drive east on I-64. Just past Winchester, bear right on the Bert T. Combs Mountain Parkway (exit #98). Get off at exit #33. Turn left on KY 11 and then right on KY 15 S. Travel 3.3 miles. Turn left on Tunnel Ridge Road and drive another 3.7 miles. Just past the wood fence, the gravel road dead-ends into the Auxier Ridge parking area.

The trail offerings on Tunnel Ridge Road beckon you like the beer selection at your favorite microbrewery. Gray's Arch. Sandstone. Paleo. Pinch-em Tight. Which to try now? Which to try later? Which to save for your next visit? It's a wonderful dilemma, though it's hard to choose. This hike utilizes two trails——Auxier Ridge and Courthouse Rock——to make a loop hike.

Courthouse Rock

Auxier Ridge Trail

Courthouse Rock Trail

TH

Tunnel Ridge Rd.

Auxier Ridge Trail (#204) is an excellent choice regardless of the time of year. The trail, traversing ridges and saddles composed of sandstone and limestone, is always well-drained after a heavy spring rain. Summer foliage showcases the undulating knobs and mountains of the Gorge, before the autumn's warm colors give way to winter's silent outcroppings of far-away ridges.

Begin your journey at the trailhead just off the parking area. A quick descent through the hardwood canopy provides a fast lesson in forest recovery. The most recent run-away campfire and pine-beetle damage has left its mark on much of Auxier Ridge. Though a bit disheartening at times, the fire damage is belittled by nature's perseverance to reforest itself. Spring hikers will marvel at the pink and yellow Lady's Slippers emergence from the charred surroundings, as the newly hatched rhododendron and maple leaves keep pace. May's flush of pink and white mountain laurel will soon be followed by the wild blueberries of midsummer.

In less than a mile, Courthouse Rock Trail will come in on your left. To walk this loop counter-clockwise, stay on the high road, as Auxier Ridge only gets better. (You will return to this intersection when you complete the Courthouse Rock Trail.) Bear right at the fork, following the white diamond blazes. High on the ridge, be sure to hold the hands of young children, old dogs, and those prone to suddenly breaking out in tango. Haystack Rock will soon be on your left, with Double Arch off in the distance. Shortly before reaching Courthouse Rock, you'll see the trail follow several flights of stairs quickly descending to your left. Don't bother waiting for the elevator.

It's easy to lose time scrambling the rocks at the base of Courthouse Rock. The trail continues to your left, although changing name to Courthouse Rock Trail (#202). A short quarter-mile hike will lead you to the intersection of #202 and the trail to Double Arch. Bearing left (staying on Courthouse Rock Trail) will complete the loop and return you to the Auxier Ridge parking area. Alternately, the 1.75-mile trail to Double Arch (one-way) is available for the hardy hiker.

Courthouse Rock Trail continues through a hemlock, oak and rhododendron forest. A careful eye might spot a Yellow Lady's Slipper or two, bluets, or ground pine. The ferns grow quite thick here and provide a luscious groundcover much of the year. For the most part, the 2-plus mile trail follows the base of Auxier Ridge. A steep ascent will bring you back to the top of Auxier Ridge. Turn right and in less than a mile you will be back to your vehicle.

Side Trip:
On your way back out on Tunnel Ridge Road, stop at the large parking lot and picnic area on your left for Gray's Arch. A one-mile hike will lead you to one of the prettiest arches in the Gorge. An easy 0.2-mile walk on Gray's Arch Trail (#205) will connect with only a slightly more difficult Rough Trail (#221). A staircase will afford you a closer look at the arch.

44 Rock Bridge / Swift Camp Creek Trail

A hemlock- and rhododendron-lined path, leading to the only waterfall arch in Kentucky.

Trail Length: 1.4 to 10.5 miles

Facilities: Pit toilets and picnic tables at the trailhead. No drinking water available.

Hours: Be off the trail by dark.

Additional Information: Overnight backpackers must obtain a permit.

Directions: Drive east on I-64. Just past Winchester, bear right on the Bert T. Combs Mountain Parkway (exit #98). Get off on exit #40, at the sign for Beattyville. Turn right on KY 15. Drive 0.7 miles, and then take another right on KY 715. In 0.4 miles you will see a gravel road on your right and a sign to Rock Bridge Picnic Area on your left. A right-hand turn and three miles of gravel road will take you to the picnic area and trailhead.

This trail is frequently touted as *"If you only hike one trail in the Red River Gorge, this should be the one"*…. And we're not going to argue with that. This hike is a popular spot for day trippers on a Sunday afternoon, and a starting point for seasoned backpackers looking for a little more solitude.

The Rock Bridge Nature Trail (#207) is a loop trail beginning and ending on either side of the picnic area. Most people would probably find it easier to walk counterclockwise by starting at the trailhead sign and finishing close to where the bathrooms are located. After leaving the parking area, the paved trail begins a steep descent that includes several short sets of stairs, many of them carved into the soft sandstone. A large rockhouse will appear on your right, as the trail bears left. Be sure to take a little time exploring the rockhouse, whether cool water drips amongst the summer ferns or icicles pay homage to Old Man Winter. Any time of year, this is a pretty cool place to be.

The trail continues along a wide path under towering hemlocks along Rockbridge Fork creek until you hear the sound of Creation Falls. A small trail spur will allow for better views and ample picture taking. A short distance further along the path leads you to Rock Bridge, just below the confluence of Rockbridge Fork and Swift Camp Creek. Rock Bridge is just one of many of Mother Nature's engineering marvels. For countless years the creek has flowed over and beneath the layers of sandstone, eroding the softer rock while leaving a spectacular arch spanning the water. This type of formation over water is referred to as a 'waterfall arch.'

A small wooden footbridge and a few stairs will lead you to one end of Rock Bridge. While climbing on rock arches is strictly forbidden in the Gorge, this is one spot where everyone tends to flagrantly disregard the rule of law.

For many hikers this is their final destination before heading back up to the parking lot. The trail continues past Rock Bridge and in another 75 yards you'll see the sign showing you the way back to your vehicle. Take a left here to complete the Rock Bridge Trail loop. The climb up has several resting places, some with beautiful views off to your left.

If a longer hike is what you're looking for, at the trail sign stay straight on the path, which becomes Swift Camp Creek Trail (#219). From this juncture you could hike another 3 miles to Turtle Falls (a large rockhouse); 4.5 miles to Wildcat Trail;

or 6.5 miles to highway 715 and other Red River Gorge trails. These distances are one way so make sure you do the math correctly.

Regardless of which option you choose, Swift Camp Creek Trail will not fail to enchant those who travel this path. Spring hikers will be rewarded with lively waterfalls and the sounds of the creek below. You'll be hard-pressed to find enough wood nymphs for all the pink lady's slippers lining the trail. Early summer brings the white and pale pink blooms of the rhododendron and the shimmery white flowers of the magnolias into their glory. And fall and winter hikers will marvel at the plethora of rock houses along Swift Camp Creek, whose number would dwarf those found in Chevy Chase and Ashland combined.

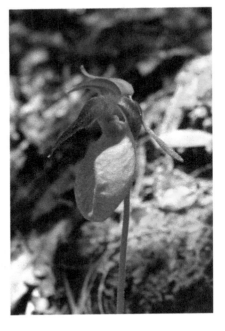

If you elect to continue on Swift Camp Creek Trail, hiking to Turtle Falls and back to the Rock Bridge picnic area will result in a total of approximately 7.5 miles. Alternately, you could hike Swift Camp Creek Trail to the turn-off for Wildcat Trail and back to the parking area for a total of almost 10.5 miles. Both of these estimates include the Rock Bridge loop of 1.4 miles.

Another option would be to leave a shuttle vehicle on KY 715 at the Angel Windows/ Swift Camp Creek parking lot. This parking lot is 3.3 miles further down KY 715 from where you turned off on the gravel Rock Bridge Road. By leaving a shuttle vehicle you can walk both the Rock Bridge Trail and the Swift Creek Trail for a total of 7.25 miles (assuming you only hike one-half of the Rock Bridge loop). For this option you may want a better trail and road map, unless endowed with a huge cache of faith in your orienteering skills.

Side Trip:

The Angel Windows Trail leaves directly from the parking lot of the same name, with directions given above. A short quarter-mile hike brings you to a set of small double arches. Don't let the kids think McDonald's has a monopoly on this phenomenon.

45 Sky Bridge Trailapalooza

An introduction to the sights, history, and culture of Red River Gorge.

Trail Length: 2 miles

Facilities: Bathrooms and drinking water at visitors center; pit toilets at some trailheads.

Hours: Visitors center is open daily, 9 am-5:30 pm. Be off the trail by dark.

Additional Information: Overnight backpackers must obtain a permit.

Directions: Drive east on I-64. Just past Winchester, take exit #98 for the Bert T. Combs Mountain Parkway. Stay on the Parkway until Slade, exit #33. Turn left on KY 11 and another left on KY 15.

This "hike" involves as much driving as it does walking, but is designed to give the first-time visitor an overview of the Gorge while keeping the hiking time to short, easy trails. Highlights include Nada Tunnel, the Gladie Cultural-Environmental Learning Center, Sky Bridge, Whistling Arch, and Angel Windows.

After turning left on KY 15, drive 1.5 miles before taking a right on KY 77 (at the small community of Nada). About 2 miles down this road you will encounter Nada Tunnel. Finished in 1911, the 900' railroad tunnel was built by the Dana Lumber Company to haul logs out of the Red River area. (Transpose the letters of 'Dana' and see what you get.) There is a small spring on the right that locals use to fill their water jugs, and another pull-off just past that if you want to read the sign and take pictures. Be sure to turn your headlights on before entering the tunnel.

Drive another 3.5 miles past the tunnel, bearing right on KY 715, to get to the Gladie Cultural-Environmental Learning Center. The visitor's center is a great way to learn more about the geology, history, and culture of the Gorge. Multiple exhibits showcase how the natural arches were formed, while the younger kids can learn how to make their very own arrow and arrowhead. From exhibits on banjo music to wildflower identification to the early pioneers who settled this valley, Gladie is definitely worth a stop on your tour.

Upon leaving Gladie, turn right on KY 715. Drive another 4.8 miles to the turn-off for Sky Bridge. The 0.8-mile road to the parking lot includes several scenic overlooks. The trailhead for Sky Bridge arch is at the end of the lot. The first part of the trail is paved and takes you immediately to the top of the arch. Watch your step here, as the arch is quite narrow and the drop-off quite steep. At the opposite end of the bridge the trail continues another 0.75 miles below the arch and back to the parking lot. Near the toilets is another paved road leading to a scenic overlook. Parking is extremely limited here, although it does include a dedicated handicap spot. A short paved path takes you to a view of Sky Bridge and Swift Camp Creek.

To continue your tour of Red River Gorge, go back out Sky Bridge Road, turning right on KY 715. In just a few tenths of a mile you will see the parking lot for Whistling Arch on your right. This short easy trail leads you to a large rockhouse with a small arch on one end. The trail continues a short distance on the other side of the arch to more scenic overlooks.

Leaving the parking area for Whistling Arch, turn right and drive 0.7 miles to the parking area for Angel Windows. This is also a short and easy path to a group of small arches and several rockhouses. Although not the large-scale arches like Sky Bridge, Angel Windows is extremely interesting geologically and definitely fun for the kids.

From Angel Windows, turn right on KY 715 until it Ts with KY 15. A left-hand turn will take you back to the Mountain Parkway.

Side Trip:

If geocaching is your thing, there's an educational route through the Red River Gorge that is designed for kids (but great for adults, too). See geocaching.com for more information.

46 Salato Wildlife Education Center

Complete with wildlife exhibits, native plants, a fishing pond, and hiking trails, Salato is a great family outing.

Trail Length: Unpaved trails from 0.5 to 3.5 miles. Paved accessible trail follows outdoor wildlife exhibit area and is open only during nature center hours.

Facilities: Staffed nature center, outdoor wildlife exhibits, fishing lake with accessible pier, restrooms, picnic tables and shelters, grills.

Hours: Hiking trails open daily, sunrise to sunset. Trail closures possible due to special events. Pea Ridge Trail is closed the first weekend of modern gun and muzzleloader hunting seasons.

Nature center hours: Sunday and Monday, CLOSED; Tuesday–Friday, 9 am-5 pm; Saturday, 10 am-5 pm. Closed on all state holidays and Thanksgiving (Thursday - Sunday). Check the website for winter closure schedule, typically late November through early March.

Additional Information: Nature Center fees: adults $4; children 5-18 $2; under 5 free. No pets allowed. Hiking on the unpaved trails is free.

Directions: From I-64 W exit #53B, take US 127 N and travel 1.5 miles to US 60. Turn left and drive 1.7 miles west on US 60 to the entrance of the Kentucky Department of Fish and Wildlife. Turn right into the complex and proceed ahead 0.5 miles to the Salato Wildlife Education Center.

Salato can be a wonderful way to introduce your children to the outdoors. Your first stop should be the nature center replete with stuffed specimens of Kentucky's native and endangered wildlife. Birds fly overhead, fish swim in tanks (and also fly overhead, which can be a little disconcerting), and mammals live forever in their naturally contrived surroundings. The indoor exhibits are as tasteful as the live trout are purported to be.

From the rear of the building, a paved trail takes you past the outdoor exhibits, including eagles, black bear, wildcats, bison, wild turkeys, and elk.

Three hiking trails take you through native Kentucky grasslands and hardwood forests. The HabiTrek and Prairie trails can be combined to make a one-mile loop. The Pea Ridge Loop adds another 3 miles of the best scenery the park has to offer, including classic Kentucky woodlands, bubbling creeks, and quaint stone fences. A new spur off the Pea Ridge Trail takes you to the remains of the old Luttrell homestead.

The large pond is kept stocked and fishing is free for those under the age of 16. For the more mature crowd, Kentucky fishing and hunting licenses are available for sale at the Education Center. Everything is BYOB——bring your own bait. Picnic shelters and grills are available free on a first-come basis, and some can be reserved for a nominal fee.

Special programs include wildlife talks, photography workshops, birding seminars, and native plant sales. See their website for a complete list of current programs and special hours. AnimalTracks audio guides can also be borrowed at the Center, free of charge.

Side Trip:
Bring along ye ol' fishin' pole and drop a line. Add a blanket, picnic and you've got a cheap date.

Salato Wildlife Education Center
1 Sportsman's Lane
Frankfort, KY, 40601
(some navigation programs still use the old address of
1 Game Farm Rd., Frankfort, KY, 40506)
Phone: (800) 858-1549 on weekdays or (502) 564-7863 anytime
Web: http://goo.gl/OqKL3Q

47 Sally Brown Nature Preserve

A classic example of central Kentucky woodlands, tumbling creeks, and majestic palisades.

Trail Length: 2.5 miles; can easily add another 2.8 miles from trailhead.

Facilities: None.

Hours: Daily, sunrise to sunset.

Additional Information: This preserve is adjacent to the Crutcher Nature Preserve. Both trail systems start at the same trailhead. Consequently, it is very easy to hike both trails the same day.

Directions: From Lexington, travel south on US 27 (Nicholasville Road), crossing the Kentucky River into Garrard County. At the top of the hill, turn right on KY 1845 (also known as Rogers Road, the second road on the right after you cross the river). In 3.5 miles, KY 1845 Ts at the Camp Dick Fire Station. Turn left (on Polly's Bend Road) and travel 0.2 miles. Take a right at the stop sign on High Bridge Road. Go 2 miles and turn right on Bowman's Bottom Road. The road dead-ends onto private property at the Bowman Brooks House. Park in the small gravel lot on your right.

The Sally Brown Nature Preserve is comprised of 632 acres, with several hundred additional acres of protected land serving as a buffer zone, assuring pristine water quality and habitat protection for a host of rare wildflowers and mammals living in the area. This is one of those areas you hate to write about. Rarely do you see another car in the lot and even less frequently do you see another hiker along the trail——and we'd like to keep it that way. Writing about beautiful areas attracts more

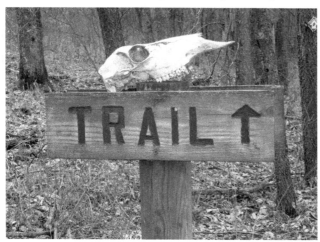

crowds, but it is precisely this growing demand for outdoor recreation that encourages a greater provisioning of parks, and the protection of Kentucky's natural beauty and rare ecosystems.

Members of the Bowman family originally settled this land, after they received multiple Revolutionary War land grants for their years of service. A portion of the preserve's trail system is along an old roadbed the Bowman brothers built for access to the river. In 2000, the original part of the Bowman Brooks House was completely restored.

The preserve was created in the early 1990s, with generous funding from Sally and W.L. Lyons Brown (of Brown-Forman fame), and one of their daughters and her husband (Mr. and Mrs. Alan M. Boyd). Born in Alaska of a US military general and his wife, Mrs. Brown was an ardent conservationist, trained artist, and well-known thoroughbred and cattle breeder. Her bio reads as a who's who in the realm of groundbreaking environmentalism both in Kentucky and around the world.

Combined with the adjacent Crutcher and Earl Wallace Nature Preserves, these three parks protect five miles of Bowman's Bend along the Kentucky River, all the way to the mouth of the Dix River. The preserves are instrumental in protecting many of the palisades (the towering cliffs of native dolomitic limestone) and the resulting fragile ecosystems found here. The area is home to many birds, such as osprey, peregrine falcon, summer tanager, and great blue heron; mammals, including bobcat and flying squirrel; and wildflowers, particularly the rare snow trillium.

To find the trailhead, pass through the fence at the end of the lot by the trail marker sign indicating the W.L. Lyons Brown Trail. Descend the hill by hugging the fence and tree line on your right, keeping the meadow to your left. A 100-yard perimeter walk will take you to another gate and another trail sign. From there you will be able to see the kiosk, complete with brochures loaded in the mail box, topo maps, and a brief history of the area. Note the trail names and mileage markers. Pay homage to the young Girl Scout who graciously made this her merit project, and you're on your way.

The W.L. Lyons Brown Trail will be to your left and the Crutcher Trail on your right. (See the entry on the Crutcher Nature Preserve for a complete description of the latter trail.) Bearing to the path on your left, you will soon come to the start of a loop trail. While you can easily go either way, hiking counterclockwise will provide the best views of the river and palisades (limestone cliffs). A small creek falls off quickly to your right, cutting a path through native Kentucky hardwoods.

The trail then runs parallel to the palisades that have formed on the south side of the river, allowing you views of the cliffs on the north side. Several footbridges carry you across small, tumbling, spring-fed creeks appearing out of nowhere. Because of the abundance of wildflowers and spectacular views of the palisades, many are partial to hiking Sally Brown in the spring. Summer foliage blocks many of the good views of the cliffs, so hiking in late fall is another option.

At the far end of the loop trail you will find a worthwhile spur following the old 1800s roadbed to the river. The trail begins a steep quarter-mile descent, allowing the palisades to loom overhead. At the bottom of the hill, note the two bat houses adjacent to the small mosquito pond on your left (rendering this portion of the hike perhaps less desirable in the summer). Standing at the river's edge the palisades are again clearly in sight and waterfowl may be seen.

After a heart-pumping walk back up the hill, bear right to continue your counterclockwise circuit and to return to the kiosk. At this juncture, you can either head right back through the fence and up the hill to your vehicle, or bear left on the Crutcher Trail.

Sally Brown Nature Preserve
Bowman's Bottom Road
Bryantsville, KY 40444
Web: http://goo.gl/zdCM2n

48 Shaker Village: The Nature Preserve

Forty miles of multi-use trails promise beautiful vistas of native grasses, intimate stone cliffs along Shawnee Run Creek, and towering palisades over the Kentucky River.

Trail Length: 1 to 6+ miles

Facilities: Gift shop serves as visitors center. Restrooms and water are available here. A one-half mile trail is handicap accessible.

Hours: Daily, sunrise to sunset

Waiver: All trail-users are required to sign a property usage waiver available at the Admission Booth, Centre Trailhead or The Inn. Free.

Dogs: Permitted only on the Village Loop, River Road Trail, and the Palisades Trail.

Additional Information: Trails are for hiking, biking and equestrian use. Mountain bikers are welcome, but must give way to hikers and horses.

Directions: From the intersection of Harrodsburg Road and Man O' War Boulevard, travel southwest on US 68 W. After crossing the Kentucky River, climb the hill until you see Shaker Village on your right and KY 33 on your left. The total distance from the intersection at Man O' War to Shaker Village is 19.4 miles.

Shaker Village has made huge strides in turning 3,000 acres of "original Shaker countryside" into a Nature Preserve complete with hiking trails, historic mills, tumbling creeks, bird blinds, and stone fences. What a find, only 40 minutes from Lexington and free for most outdoors enthusiasts (equestrian users are requested to pay a small fee for trailer parking, boarding, and running water.)

Although trail maps are available from their website, you can also pick one up at Shaker Village. The maps are quite large and show an appreciable amount of detail. All visitors should sign in at the Ticket and Information Office (the gift shop) or at any of the new trailhead kiosks. After signing a waiver, pick up your map and head out to one of three trailhead parking sites. Most of the trails are loops, and are rated easy or moderate.

Trailhead Parking Lot 1 has some of the best access to the wooded areas of the Preserve and easy access to several of the historical sites, bird blinds, and most other trails. A popular hike is piecing the Towering Sycamore Trail with the Shawnee Run and Heritage Trails to create a scenic 6-mile loop (shown on the accompanying map). If you haven't already, sign in at the kiosk near the Loetscher Bird Blind.

From the kiosk, walk northeast on the paved road, passing over the bridge of Shawnee Run Creek. Take the mowed trail off to your right that leads to the

Towering Sycamore Trail (do not turn left on the connector trail). This is a shared use trail and you may see horses and carriages traveling the same path. A short ten-minute walk brings you to the site of an old fulling mill used in wool processing, circa 1822. Signage provides a description and additional pictures of the mill.

Shortly after the mill, the Towering Sycamore Trail joins with Shawnee Run Trail. Go right (north) to complete the loop. The Shawnee Run Trail passes through a short grassy area before rejoining the creek. Both the Towering Sycamore and Shawnee Run Trails cross Shawnee Run Creek multiple times and are quite beautiful. The area is spectacular in the late autumn when the fallen leaves expose the limestone bluffs along Shawnee Run Creek, or in winter when icefalls form on either side of the creek. However, a few words of caution: Water levels can make some of these creek crossings very difficult for those on foot or wheel. Moving part of your hike to higher ground on the Chinquapin Trail might prove to be a wise option for those wanting dry feet on cold days.

From here the Shawnee Run Trail stays in the trees above the creek, before climbing up a short hill to open pasture. Bear right at the picnic table. You should be about 2.7 miles from the trailhead. If you have the energy, be sure to add on the half-mile Chinn-Poe spur for spectacular spring wildflower displays of wood poppies, trout lilies, rue anemone, and more.

Climbing back up the Chinn-Poe Trail, turn right (west) on the Shawnee Run Trail. From here the trail passes through open pasture, laced with old fencerows. The finches truly seem to enjoy the views of bucolic farmland. When the trail turns east again, you'll pass a stand of native cane and several patches of prickly pear.

At the end of a diagonal rock fence, take a hairpin turn to your right and hook up with the Heritage Trail. The path leads you over an old Shaker mill and past several other historic sites. A left at the Quail Restoration sign will bring you back to the Loetscher Bird Blind.

The equestrian crowd primarily uses the trailhead at Parking Lot 2, although anyone can park there. Several trails can be accessed from this lot including the West Lot, Chinquapin, Shawnee Run, Anderson, and Quail Hollow loops. Trailhead Parking Lot 3 is next to Shaker Village itself, and offers access to the Tanyard Trail loop. Short connector trials are abundant in the preserve and allow for multiple options to shorten or lengthen your day.

Many of the paved and gravel roads are perfect for those cycling with a watchful eye. Blind turns and narrow roads could make that next meeting an eventful one. Likewise, many of the trails are also well suited for mountain biking, although notable exceptions include the Chinn-Poe, Heritage, and River Road Trails. It's highly unusual for a preserve to allow bicyclists, so don't wear out your welcome.

Shaker Village is to be applauded for trying to accommodate a wide range of outdoor lovers. However, that requires us all to be on our best behavior. Hikers and bicyclists should yield to equestrians at all times. When horses approach, quietly move far off the trail and cyclists should dismount. Talk in low tones to the horses and riders so those huge beasts know where you are. This is not the time to find out who has the biggest shoes.

Side Trip:
At Shaker Village, the Dixie Belle riverboat is available for passengers on a seasonable basis. Private canoeists and kayakers are also welcome at Shaker Landing. Bring a clean shirt and change of shoes for some fine dining at Shaker Village. Reservations may be required. Of course, you may also want to take a tour of Shaker Village itself.

The Nature Preserve at Shaker Village
Shaker Village of Pleasant Hill
3501 Lexington Road
Harrodsburg, KY 40330
Phone: (800) 734-5611
Web: shakervillageky.org/recreation

49 Skullbuster: Scott County Adventure Trails

Keep your eye on this one. Lots of potential open to hikers, trail runners, mountain bikers, and equestrians.

Trail Length: 7.8 miles and growing
Facilities: None. Also be sure to bring plenty of water.
Hours: Daily, sunrise to sunset.
Additional Information: Scott County purchased this property several years ago with the hopes of one day building a water reservoir. That plan has been put on hold. Equestrians have long used this park, but bikers and hikers are the relative newcomers. Requests have been made not to post trail maps or other information on the Internet.
Directions: Head north on I-75. Take exit #126 (US 62). Turn left on Cherry Blossom Way, toward Georgetown. Travel 0.5 miles; turn right on KY 32 E (Champion Way, which becomes Long Lick Pike). Drive 9.4 miles and take a right on Skinnerburg Road. Go 2 miles. Turn left on Stockdell Road. Park in the small gravel lot on your left as indicated by the red and white signs with arrows and KyMBA stickers. You will see two other large signs posted No Trespassing By Order of Scott Fiscal Court. It's ok to park your vehicle here.

Helmets off to the Scott County government for buying this 1600-acre chunk of central Kentucky woodlands, and to the Kentucky Mountain Bike Association (KyMBA) for building some mighty fine trails. The park itself goes by the name of Scott County Adventure Trails. The newly-crafted set of biking and hiking trails were named for the now defunct community of Skullbuster and the meat slaughtering facility located there.

The first biking and hiking trails were completed in 2010 using incredible amounts of volunteer labor and thoughtful discussions with the equestrian community. Long-term plans call for additional waves of trail building in subsequent years. We like that kind of vision.

After parking in the lot, hike up Stockdell Road along Lytles Fork for about 0.3 miles until you see an old red farm gate blocking the road, and a large sign posted *PRIVATE PROPERTY KEEP OUT By Order of Scott Fiscal Court*. Hikers and bikers can simply go around the locked gate through the small entrance by the trail sign. The posted trail map has become rather dated, but the trails themselves are very well-marked. The sign also includes some good information about rules for using the park. Please read these carefully.

Wisely, equestrian riders use separate trails from the mountain bikers and caution signs are posted in the few places where the two types of trails intersect. Hikers and trail runners are permitted to use both the biking and the horse trails.

For a mixed-use park of this type, trail etiquette is paramount. Mountain bikers must give way to hikers and trail runners. However, this writer finds it relatively easy to step aside for the bikers, particularly since that group was so instrumental in making these trails a reality.

Hikers should give way to horses on the equestrian trails. Quietly step off the trail and continue talking in a low voice, so both the horse and the rider know where you are at all times. However, the equestrian trails in this part of the park are lightly used and are in excellent condition at time of publishing.

To access the trails, continue walking up Stockdell Road another 0.4 miles. You'll see a trail come in on your left, boldly blazed in green and another KyMBA sign (and one marked 'No horses'). If you walk up Stockdell Road another 100 yards, an equestrian trail begins on your left, right at the old wooden fence pole and just before the road crosses a small creek. No signs or blazes are posted but you will see the trail.

If you take the green trail, you will hike 0.7 miles before it Ts into the blue trail. The 5-mile blue trail is a vortex of twists, turns, loops, and switchbacks—— a true test for anyone's sense of direction. However, the blue trail is basically one big loop and very easy to navigate. You can go left or right at this junction and return to this same spot from the other direction. In total you

can hike 1.4 miles from your vehicle to get to the blue trail; loop around 5 miles; and another 1.4 miles brings you back to the parking lot, for a total of 7.8 miles.

Two new trails were finished in 2011; the 1.7 mile orange trail (which is slightly steeper and more technical than the other trails) and the white (or gray) connector trails have been expanded. The heavy spring rains of 2011 significantly slowed trail building activity. However, these trails were built to International Mountain Biking Standards and are in excellent condition. The mountain biking community is proud of their work.

The terrain itself is mostly rolling hills, covered with third or fourth growth Kentucky hardwoods (beech, oak, hickory, maple, and buckeye) with a few small cedar thickets. Deer, wild turkey, fox, and other small mammals seem to have the run of the place. As a result, the ecosystem is classic central Kentucky with a few noteworthy highlights.

Several area bike shops were instrumental in getting the volunteers geared up for this huge undertaking. And obviously they had fun. The trails are fast, moderately technical, and laced with humor. We hope to see more in the future.

Side Trip:

After hiking or riding, take KY 32 E back towards Georgetown. A right on US 25 will bring you to Elkhorn Creek. Have a bite to eat creekside, imbibe in a cold drink, and enjoy the sound of falling water.

Skullbuster

Skinnerburg Road
Stamping Ground, KY 40379

50 Tom Dorman State Nature Preserve

An old stage coach trail leading to scenic views of the Kentucky River palisades.

Trail Length: 1.9 to 2.6 miles
Facilities: None
Hours: Daily, sunrise to sunset
Directions: From Lexington, head south on Nicholasville Road (US 27). Bear right on the Nicholasville by-pass, continuing south until you cross the Kentucky River. Once across the bridge, travel 1 mile. Turn right on KY 1845. Drive another mile. Turn right on Jess Brim Road, at the Tom Dorman Nature Preserve sign. Continue straight for another 0.7 miles, following the signs. The road dead-ends into the parking lot on your right.

Just south of Jessamine County lies a pretty little nature preserve filled with several rare wildflowers, and more than 25 species of mammals and 35 of the reptilian sort. Comprised of over 800 acres, the preserve straddles both sides of the Kentucky River, but due to the fragile ecosystem and steep cliffs, only the southern (Garrard County) portion is open to the public. Most of the funding for this preserve came from the Kentucky River Authority (KRA), the Nature Conservancy, and yes, those nature plates so many of us flaunt. Tom was the former director and chairman of the KRA and instrumental in creating the preserve.

The small parking lot always has room for you, promising uncluttered trails and quiet wanderings. Be sure to sign in, as headcounts are important. The kiosk has some information about Kentucky's state nature preserves and a trail map posted on the sign. You may also want to download your own map, replete with mileage markings, from their website.

The trail system at Tom Dorman is like a one-armed snowman from Calvin and Hobbes (please forgive us Bill Watterson): one large loop (the body) and a short spur (left arm), both of which are supporting a smaller loop (the head). Regardless, the trail takes you past some of the oldest exposed rock in Kentucky, 450 million year old Ordovician limestone. It's nice to feel young again.

Beginning your hike clockwise has two advantages: the palisade views are better as you head up river and the steep descent to the river is facilitated with natural limestone ledges and hand-hewn steps. The trail loops under nut trees aplenty (oak, buckeye, and shagbark hickory), past multiple crevasses and sinkholes, and around the occasional Kentucky-style tarn. But be forewarned: After a heavy rain, multiple creek crossings will test those new Gore-Tex boots.

The lucky hiker may catch sight of an eight-point buck or one of the many red-tailed hawks circling overhead. It's not unusual to be heralded by the squawking of a great heron announcing your arrival to the riverbank. In the month of May, hikers might find themselves surrounded by gently falling fluff from the great cottonwoods towering overhead. In late summer be on the lookout for an abundance of paw paw or mulberry near the trail. And a profusion of mayapple, jewelweed, bloodroot, and wild ginger can be found underfoot.

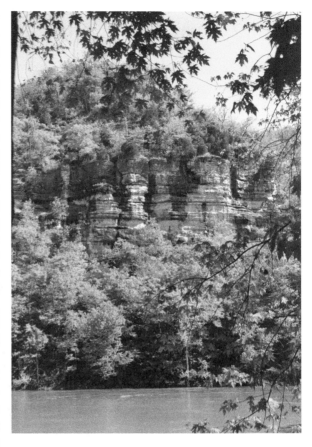

The return back up from the river follows an old stage-coach road from what was once Knights Ferry. Back at the parking lot, be sure to spot the bundle of mistletoe overhead in the branches of the walnut tree. It's a great time to steal that kiss or remember one from days long past.

Side Trip:
If time and energy levels permit, consider adding another trail or two in the vicinity from the Jim Beam, Sally Brown, or Crutcher Nature Preserves.

Tom Dorman State Nature Preserve
Jess Brim Road
Lancaster, KY 40444
**Web: naturepreserves.ky.gov/naturepreserves/
Pages/tomdorman.aspx**

51 Vanhook Falls

A relatively easy trail with multiple waterfalls and scenic views.

Trail Length: 5.4 miles roundtrip
Facilities: None available.
Hours: None posted.
Additional Information: Dogs are permitted off–leash. There are several good overnight camping spots in the area.
Directions: From I-75 south, take exit #38 for London. Turn right (west)

onto KY 192. Drive 14 miles to the intersection of KY 192 W and KY 1193 S. A large gravel parking lot will be on your left. Park here and carefully cross back over KY 192 to the north side of the road. The trail follows a portion of the Sheltowee Trace #100.

It's no wonder that Vanhook Falls is popular with locals and city-folk alike. The trail passes under lush, towering hemlocks as it makes its way along scenic Pounder Branch of Cane Creek. With the exception of the last 100 yards, the trail is wide and flat to rolling. And the distance can easily be increased with the multitude of longer trail options in the immediate vicinity. Despite all of these alluring attributes, the trail to Vanhook Falls is typically quiet and peaceful most of the time.

The 40-foot Vanhook Falls lies in the heart of the nearly 6,700-acre Cane Creek Wilderness Management Area in the Daniel Boone National Forest. Several smaller tributaries, including Rooks, Laurel, Upper and Lower Pounder, Vanhook, and Grassy Branches, all converge in the Cane Creek drainage before flowing into the Rockcastle River.

However, if water is what you're looking for, and waterfalls in particular, this hike is best done in the spring or after a heavy rain. But with lots of spring-fed creeks and interesting rock formations, even a winter hike is worthwhile.

Once you've parked, carefully cross back over KY 192 to find the trailhead. As mentioned above, the trail follows along a portion of the Sheltowee Trace #100, so look for signage indicating such. After a slight descent through oak, hickory, and beech trees, the trail quickly picks up Pounder Branch on the right and the vegetation evolves into more of a hemlock and rhododendron ecosystem. Be on the alert for smaller waterfalls as the trail crosses several other minor tributaries, and weaves back and forth across Pounder Branch.

Hike north along the Sheltowee Trace #100 for approximately 2 miles until you reach a small sandstone outcropping. Here the trail takes a brief, but steep descent into the confluence of Pounder Branch and Cane Creek, with two wooden footbridges crossing each in turn. The large flat rocks along Cane Creek make a beautiful lunch spot overlooking the lively rapid where the footbridge crosses over. From this vantage point, the placid Cane Creek begins pouring through large boulder gardens, as it tumbles into the Rockcastle River another two miles downstream.

Cross over Cane Creek and walk another 0.1 miles along the Sheltowee Trace and begin a slow ascent up the Vanhook Branch drainage. The trail follows under a nice rock overhang before climbing swiftly to a good view of Vanhook Falls. A spur trail then drops down to the base of the falls, allowing hikers lots of beautiful photo ops. You can also scramble up behind the falls, allowing the falling water to partially obstruct views of the creek drainage below.

After oohing and awing sufficiently, return to the main trail and bear left to hike above the falls. The creek above the falls also provides some pretty views of the drainage. From here you can retrace your steps back to the parking lot or follow the suggestions below.

Trail Map: http://goo.gl/ZcysjN

Side Trip:
If you have lots of energy for an even longer day hike, or have a backpack outfitted for an overnighter, after viewing Vanhook Falls, continue north along the Sheltowee Trace #100 for another mile. The Rockcastle Narrows East Trail #401 splits to the northwest as the Sheltowee continues heading northeast. Bear left (NW) on trail #401.

The Rockcastle Narrows East Trail is a 5-mile loop that will take you down to the Rockcastle River, up along Cane Creek, past the hidden remains of the old Warner Hotel, and back to just above Vanhook Falls. You can then follow the Sheltowee Trace #100 south back to the parking lot. This "lollipop" trail configuration will take you about 10 miles. There are a few good camping spots along the river and one just west of Vanhook Falls and north of the Rockcastle Narrows East Trail.

Trail map: http://goo.gl/HBci5I

Stearns Ranger District
3320 Hwy. 27 North
Whitley City, KY 42653
Phone: (606) 376-5323
Web: http://goo.gl/4vTsfc

52 Veterans Memorial Wildlife Management Area

Almost 2500 acres of rolling hills, hardwood forests and open pasture.

Trail Length: Varies; none marked.
Facilities: None available.
Hours: Dawn to dusk.
Additional Information: Be sure to check the web site of the Kentucky Department of Fish and Wildlife Resources for dates of the hunting and bow seasons so you don't become part of someone's quota. Dogs are permitted off-leash.

Directions: Follow I-75 north of Georgetown. Take exit # 129 (KY 620 E or Cherry Blossom Way). Turn left (west) and drive 0.7 miles. Turn right (north) on US 25. Drive another 1.7 miles. Turn right (east) on KY 620 W or Rogers Gap Road, crossing back under I-75. The entrance to the property is immediately on your left.

Veterans Memorial WMA does not have beautiful waterfalls, majestic palisades or amazing natural arches—but what it does have is lots of wide-open space and easy access. Located about 20 minutes north of Lexington, Veterans is part of the original 6,000-acre Hall farm. Opened in summer 2012, the land is managed (like most WMAs) for the wildlife and not necessarily for you or I. No formal trails have been developed and hikers are left to wander the old farm roads and mowed pathways through open pasture and wooded areas.

Although three-quarters of Veterans WMA remains forested, corn and millet continues to be planted for the wildlife that stop here on their annual migratory paths or the full-time mammals and birds that reside here. In addition to a large number of resident deer, both wild turkeys and scarlet tanagers seem to have the run of the place.

The best hiking can be had at the far end of the property. Although the noise from I-75 is less than endearing, walking east brings some respite as the hills and trees form natural sound barriers. A small pond is also located nearby, promising largemouths, cats, and bluegill for the patient angler. KY Fish and Wildlife has also invested heavily in improving the riparian zone adjacent to the pond and several of the creeks—it will be interesting to see what this place looks like in another ten or twenty years.

Side Trip:
Since there are no designated trails, this place offers a great opportunity to hone your orienteering skills. Buy a good compass (if you don't already have one) and find a nice topo map of the area. Search the Internet for some good videos or tutorials on navigation and you're golden.

If you're hungry for some smoked brisket or a gourmet burger, stop by Sergeant's Galley on the way back to the interstate. Find them at 2176 Cincinnati Road, Georgetown, KY 40324. Closed Sundays. sergeantsgalley.com

Veterans Memorial Wildlife Management Area
Rogers Gap Road
Georgetown, KY 40324
Phone: (859) 428-2262
Web: http://goo.gl/iEPr51

53 Veterans Park

A wooded trail and a paved path wind though a large suburban park situated along West Hickman Creek.

Trail Length: 3.4 miles
Facilities: Bathrooms and water are available in season, picnic shelter, 18-hole professional disc golf course, playground, 6 baseball fields and 3 soccer/football fields.
Hours: Daily, sunrise to sunset.

Directions: From the intersection of Tates Creek Road and Man O' War Boulevard, go south 0.4 miles. Turn right on Clearwater Way, left on Southpoint Drive, and left at the US Army tank guarding the entrance to Veterans Park.

At 235 acres, Veterans Park is one of Lexington's larger recreational areas. In addition to the ball fields, the park is popular for its trails through lightly wooded areas. The main trail can be accessed at a variety of points, most of them leading to the eastern park boundary along Hickman Creek.

The park is adjacent to Lexington's West Hickman Creek Wastewater Treatment Plant, a 269-acre site in southern Fayette County. Many of the trails wander over the boundary lines between the two publicly-owned areas. Surprisingly, there are no signs indicating said property lines or indications that park users should restrict their activities.

The main 2-mile wooded trail runs the perimeter of the park and is roughly parallel to much of the disc golf course (and sandwiched between the creek and the golf course). A shorter 1.4-mile paved path runs between the ball fields and the woods.

The wooded trail is extremely popular after work and on weekends with city dwellers walking their dogs and mountain bikers spinning their wheels. Those electing to hike the trails on the southwestern side of the park will end up on old farm roads that culminate with views of Brannon Crossing in Jessamine County. Here the summer fields are filled with blackberries and chiggers competing for the same space.

Veterans Park
650 Southpoint Drive
Lexington, KY 40515
Phone: (859) 288-2900
Web: lexingtonky.gov/index.aspx?page=198

54 War Fork Creek and Resurgence Cave

Part of the Sheltowee Trace, the trail parallels War Fork Creek to the point where the creek reappears from the mouth of the cave.

Trail Length: 5 miles, round-trip

Facilities: Bathrooms are seasonally available at Turkey Foot Campground. No water available anytime.

Hours: none posted

Directions: Head south on I-75 to Berea exit #76. Turn left (east) on KY 21, traveling 1.5 miles to downtown Berea. Continue straight on KY 21 for another 5 miles until it Ts into US 421. Turn right on 421. Stay on 421 for 18.5 miles, passing through the small towns of Big Hill, Sand Gap, and Waneta, until you get to McKee. Take a left on KY 89 and travel another 3.1 miles. Make a right on Macedonia Road; drive another half-mile; then make a left on Turkey Foot Road (also known as Pilgrim's Rest Road). You should see a sign for Turkey Foot National Forest Recreation Area. In about a mile, the paved road turns to gravel. Drive an additional two miles and turn left just prior to the bridge.

This is Elsam Fork Road or Forest Development Road (FDR) 345. Heed the flood prone area signs, as you must cross a small creek bed.

On the other side of the creek find a place to park on the right shoulder, just prior to the entrance of Turkey Foot Campground. You should now be at the intersection of Elsam Fork Road (FDR 345), Girl Scout Road on your right (which takes you into the campground), and Sheltowee Trace Trail No. 100 (which at this point is actually a wide dirt path, popular amongst the ATV crowd). The trailhead is on your left, where the trail climbs a short embankment and is marked with a Sheltowee Trace NRT 100 sign.

Whew. Despite these lengthy directions, this trail is slightly over one-hour from Lexington and relatively easy to find.

The War Fork Trail is a section of the Sheltowee Trace that lies just north of McKee. The Sheltowee Trace Trail runs 282-miles from Rowan County in eastern Kentucky to Pickett State Park in northern Tennessee. Named after Daniel Boone, Sheltowee was his adopted Shawnee name meaning "Big Turtle."

The War Fork Trail follows War Fork Creek from Turkey Foot Campground to Resurgence Cave. Over the eons, this creek bed has fallen victim to Kentucky's

Resurgence Cave

Elsam Fork Rd. (FDR 345)

War Fork
Creek

FDR 345

Turkey Foot
Campground

ATV Trail

TH

karst geology that has created sinkholes, caves, and disappearing waterways across the Bluegrass. As layers of limestone bedrock have eroded, the beautiful War Fork Creek periodically travels underground, only to reappear later downstream. While this effect is not so noticeable during the spring, as summer progresses less of the creek is visible above ground. When the water does reappear, it is a cool and fresh 54 degrees.

To begin your hike, find the aforementioned Sheltowee Trail marker and begin a short, but steep climb up a reinforced embankment (erosion control for those ATVers). In 5-10 minutes of walking, the single-track War Fork Trail bears to your right as the ATV doublewide path bears left. Look for the white turtle blazes that indicate you are hiking along part of the Sheltowee Trace.

The trail roughly parallels Elsam Fork Road (FDR 345), with some interesting rock formations on your left. In a little over a mile, the trail crosses back over the road. Walk the hairpin curve on the road until you see the trail disappear again off to your right. In another mile you will cross over an old logging road. Dogleg to your right and you'll see the trail pick up again on your left. The path then descends toward War Fork Creek.

For the wildflower lovers amongst us, spring hikers will be rewarded with hillsides of trillium, mayapple, Solomon's seal, wild ginger, and maidenhair fern. Although traditionally made into cough syrup as a popular herbal remedy, maidenhair fern was also thought to "cure" male pattern baldness (neither of these cures we suggest trying at home).

Once the trail reaches the creek, Resurgence Cave is embedded in the creek bank on your left. Even during the heat of late summer, cool air arises from deep beneath the ground as the water rejoins War Fork Creek. If water levels are low enough, you can ford the creek to find a nice campsite on the other side. Here the trail continues on or you can stop for a bite of lunch, before backtracking to your vehicle.

Side Trip:
Free to campers and popular amongst locals, Turkey Foot Campground is a beautiful spot for picnicking or overnighters. The 20 camping sites are available on a first-come, first-served basis. The deep pool adjacent to the picnic area is the perfect place to wet a line in search of that elusive trout or two.

War Fork Creek @ Turkey Foot Campground
Elsam Fork Road (FDR 345)
McKee, KY 40447
**Web: www.fs.fed.us/r8/boone/documents/
rogs/sheltpdf/02turk.pdf**

55 Waterfall Chasing: Jackson and Lee Counties

Wait for the heavy spring rains and then enjoy the bounty from the heavens as you complete this circuit of Alcorn Branch, Flat Lick, and McCammon Branch Falls.

Trail Length: 3 miles for all 3 waterfalls

Facilities: Picnic tables are available at McCammon Branch.

Hours: Basically sunrise to sunset.

Additional Information: Dogs are permitted, but please clean up after them and keep them safe. They don't call them 'falls' for nothing.

Directions: The directions below will route you from I-75, just north of Richmond, KY, to all three waterfalls using a clockwise rotation.

Richmond to Alcorn Branch Falls: You want to drive to Arvel, KY. From I-75 on the north side of Richmond, take exit #90 to hit US 25 south (the bypass) for about 4 miles. Turn left (east) on KY 52 towards Irvine. Drive 17 miles. Once in Irvine, turn right (south) on KY 89. Drive 7 miles. Turn left on KY 1209. Drive the final 13 miles to the micro-community of Arvel. If KY 587 pops up on your right, you have gone a wee bit too far.

Alcorn Branch Falls to Flat Lick Falls: From Arvel you want to drive to Gray Hawk, KY. Continue driving south on KY 1209 for another 100 yards or so. Turn right on KY 587. From here it is about 12 miles to Grayhawk, KY, but you will want to keep heading south on KY 587, KY 34445 and KY 1071. That is, when KY 587 bears right (west), you want to stay straight on KY 3445. When KY 3445 Ts into KY 1071, you want to continue straight on KY 1071. When KY 1071 hits US 421, continue straight on Hays Road, then immediately bear left on Lower Hays Road. In about a mile you will see Flat Lick Road on your right——take this gravel road for another mile or so to the community center.

Flat Lick Falls to McCammon Branch Falls: Backtrack to US 421 by taking Flat Lick Road, and then a left on Lower Hays Road. At US 421, turn left (north) and drive for 1.4 miles. Turn left on Jackson County High School Road. Immediately bear left on Gray Hawk Community Park Road. Drive about 0.6 miles; drive past the little pony ring on your right and park near the picnic shelter on your right.

For a driving map from Richmond, KY you can go to https://goo.gl/maps/gx1Vk

The best time to plan for a day of waterfall chasing is just after the spring rains have arrived. Although the ratio of driving to hiking is not ideal, the steep hillsides of Lee and Jackson County create the opportunity to see three waterfalls on one grand circuit. So fill up your tank, pack a lunch, and hit the road.

Our first stop will be in the community of Arvel, for a 1.8-mile (roundtrip) out-and-back hike to Alcorn Branch Falls. All that remains of Arvel is a few houses, an old general store/post office, a trailer or two, and several junked cars (including three Gremlins if you haven't seen one of those in a long time!) Park on the side road near the general store—if it's open (frequently the door is left unlocked), respectfully step back in history and explore old-time shopping with a heart and soul. Don't touch, but do linger, if time permits.

The next thing to remember is that you have to *cross* the road (KY 1209) to get to the trailhead. Several sets of directions on the Internet suggest the trailhead is behind the store, but unless the Dorothy and the Wicked Witch of the West were here causing the buildings to be a spinnin', the trailhead is in front of the store, on the other side of the highway. So cross KY 1209 carefully until you see the old logging road and maybe even a sign for the Sheltowee Trace.

The trail follows an old logging road, known on some maps as Polly Sparks Road. Follow the first road uphill for about ten minutes, until it hits another old logging road. Bear left here and then you'll see a sign on your right directing you to the trail. Follow this trail, a section of the Sheltowee Trace, for about three-quarters of a mile until your can hear the falls. The best views can be found after descending the hillside near the rock shelter and then making your way back up the creek. Alcorn Branch Falls is a simple plunge-style fall, mostly spring-fed, pretty, but not spectacular. But few people go here, so it's worth seeing.

Once you have backtracked to your vehicle, follow the directions above to Grayhawk, KY. Park in the community center parking lot. Before you follow the paved trail to Flat Lick Falls, check out that log building! Or is it log? You won't be the first one fooled.

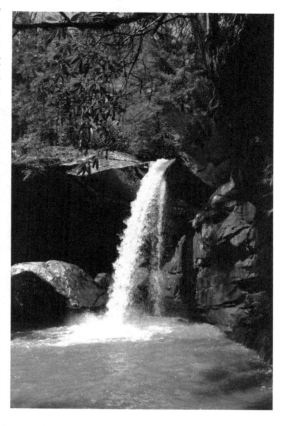

The quarter-mile paved trail takes you to a nice overlook of the plunge-style falls. The falls are simply gorgeous. You can stop and snap a few pictures, or if you're more adventurous, back up a little and take the trail just a bit higher that leads you downstream of the falls. A short descent will lead you to an old abandoned building site, a "hunting cabin" belonging to a previous landowner. From here you can walk upstream, crisscrossing the creek a few times, until you are at the base of the falls. You can either go back the way you came or scramble up the sides of the falls on creek-left and then safely cross the creek upstream of the drop. Occasionally young high-school kids jump off the falls, but it's not recommended and signage reinforces that opinion.

Once back to your vehicle, drive north on US 421 to McCammon Branch Falls, only 10-15 minutes away. After parking near the picnic shelter, take the short trail behind the shelter to a 50-yard scramble down a rather steep ravine. McCammon is more of a tiered waterfall, which changes direction as it drops. A large rockhouse provides a good vantage point or you can climb down to the base of the falls. Despite its public location, rarely do you see anyone else.

For now you're done and you can head back home, but if you have more energy, please see the Side Trip section below.

Side Trip:
If you feel like you've driven all this way and would still like to hike more, you have two other options. Just on the other side of McKee is War Fork Creek and Resurgence Cave, which can give you several more miles of hiking. Or you could swing by Anglin Falls for a 2-mile (roundtrip) hike through the John Stephenson Memorial Nature Preserve, including a gorgeous spring wildflower show of red trillium, Dutchman's breeches, white hepatica, bloodroot, and yellow trout lilies. See both of these entries elsewhere in this book.

56 Yahoo Falls and Yahoo Arch

A short hike to the tallest waterfall in Kentucky.

Trail Length: 2.5 miles, round-trip
Facilities: Bathrooms and picnic area.
Hours: Be off the trails by dusk.
Directions: Drive south on I-75. Take exit #62 (US 25) south towards KY 461 and Somerset. Follow KY 461 for 18 miles. Bear right (west) on KY 80 for 6 miles. Take a left on KY 914 W for 4.5 miles and another left on KY 1247 S for 4 miles.

Merge onto US 27 S, heading south towards Burnside and Whitley City. Follow US 27 south for 21 miles. As soon as you enter Whitley City, turn right (west) on KY 700. Drive 4 miles. Turn right on the gravel road, marked for the Yahoo Falls Picnic Area. Drive 1.5 miles further to the day-use area.

Both Yahoo Falls and Arch are located in the Big South Fork National River & Recreation Area , which straddles the Kentucky / Tennessee line. A gorgeous area, the park protects the lower reaches of the Big South Fork of the Cumberland River and many of its tributaries.

The geology of this region has created one of the highest concentrations of natural bridges in the eastern United States.

Several loop trails encircle the rockhouse that creates the 113-foot Yahoo Falls, taking you above and below the big drop for lots of great picture opportunities. Start at the parking lot and find the main trailhead, just on the other side of the bathroom. You can walk this either clockwise or counter-clockwise. Either way, the hiking area becomes a big maze, but it's easy to keep your sense of direction with the imposing structure of the rockhouse and Yahoo Creek at the bottom. If the water is low enough, you can also take the trail that leads you down the center of the creek and through some house-sized boulders. Yes, the trail takes you right though the middle of the creek——kids big and small love this!

After spending sufficient time enjoying the area around the falls, head out to Yahoo Arch Trail #602 for an out-and-back hike. From the falls, it's less than a mile to Yahoo Arch. This is really an interesting rock formation and worth seeing.

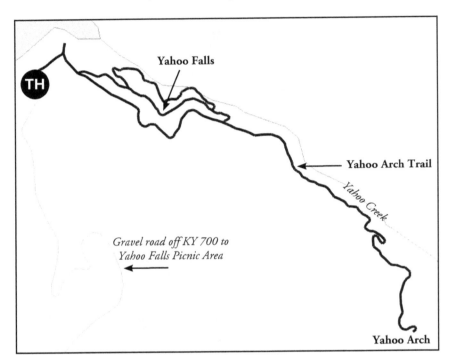

Side Trip:
About 15 miles south of Whitley City is the Blue Heron Interpretive Center, showcasing the mining and logging days of yore via old-time photographs and oral histories. Part of the BSF park, everything is free. The Visitor Center is open April 1 - October 31; 9:30 am-3:30 pm. Outdoor structures are open year-round.

The Big South Fork Scenic Railway offers train rides to Blue Heron and through the BSF gorge. For more information see bsfsry.com.

Big South Fork National River & Recreation Area
4564 Leatherwood Road
Oneida, TN 37841
Tel: (423) 569-9778
Web: http://www.nps.gov/biso
or http://goo.gl/RQaidY

57 Yahoo Loop via Negro Creek

A challenging hike that takes in both Yahoo Falls and Arch, plus scenic vistas along the Big South Fork of the Cumberland River.

Trail Length: 9.5-mile loop
Facilities: Bathrooms and picnic area.
Hours: Be off the trails by dusk.
Directions: Drive south on I-75. Take exit #62 (US 25) south towards KY 461 and Somerset. Follow KY 461 for 18 miles. Bear right (west) on KY 80 for 6 miles. Take a left on KY 914 W for 4.5 miles and another left on KY 1247 S for 4 miles. Merge onto US 27 S, towards Burnside and Whitley City. Follow US 27 south for 21 miles. As soon

as you enter Whitley City, turn right (west) on KY 700. To reach:

TH1: Drive 4 miles. Turn right on the gravel road, marked for the Yahoo Falls Picnic Area. Drive 1.5 miles to the day-use area.

TH2: Drive 3 miles. Look for the gravel, gated road FS 6003 on your left and a sign for Markers Arch on your right. Park on the gravel road.

TH3: Drive 5.5 miles, until the road deadends at Alum Ford Campground and boat ramp.

If you're up for a longer hike, this is a great option that combines sections of the Yahoo Arch Trail #602, Negro Creek Trail #612, and Sheltowee Trace Trail #100. This loop hike is located in the Big South Fork National River & Recreation Area (BSF). The park straddles the Kentucky / Tennessee line and protects the Big South Fork of the Cumberland River and many of its tributaries. The geology of the region has created one of the highest concentrations of natural bridges in the eastern United States. Many hikers like to think of the BSF as comparable to the Red River Gorge, but without all of the people.

The loop can be hiked either direction using any of three trailheads. There are pros and cons of using each: TH1 is clearly marked, parking is easy, and bathrooms are available. TH2 avoids the chaos of the picnic area in high season. And TH3 offers primitive camping at the trailhead. You can't go wrong with any of them, but the following description assumes you will start at the Yahoo Falls Picnic Area and travel clockwise.

From the far aside of the bathroom, pick up the main trailhead to Yahoo Falls. There are several small overlooks with views of the Big South Fork. At 133 feet, the falls is considered the tallest in Kentucky and is beautiful to behold any time of the year. Here the trails wrap themselves in and around a series of huge rockhouses that have formed the big drop. The lower trail goes down the center of Yahoo Creek, which if water levels permit, is a totally cool place to explore.

After spending some time walking the maze of trails, head to the far eastern side of the falls area to pick up the 0.8-mile trail to Yahoo Arch. The trail to the arch follows up along the Yahoo Creek drainage, filled with wildflowers in the spring and the greenery of hemlocks and rhododendron year-round. Yahoo Arch has a very interesting structure. While the arch itself is not that large, the landform is situated in a large bowl or depression. One can easily imagine the water swirling around eons ago, carving out the sandstone and moving tons of soil to create such a work of natural art.

From here, Yahoo Arch Trail begins a gentle climb along a ridge and soon follows an old logging road through mountain laurel and blueberry bushes. In about 1.2 miles, just before you reach KY 700, you will see a sign on your left for Marker's Arch. While the distance is relatively short (0.5 miles, one-way), the scenery is rather plain and the arch itself is not that scenic as a fallen tree has blocked much of the view.

Yahoo Arch Trail ends at KY 700. From here, turn right (west) and make a short dog-leg to pick up the 2.1-mile Negro Creek Trail on the left (south) side of the road. You'll follow the graveled and gated FS 6003 only a few yards before you see the trail straight ahead. On a recent visit, a local sheriff's political campaign sign had been used for target practice, without any indication of who won the race. Not far from the gate, the trail ducks under some power lines. Bear right (west) and look for the white diamonds blazing the trail. You'll descend a short section of steps carved into the soft sandstone as the trail begins to follow the Negro Creek drainage. Unfortunately views of the creek are scarce and sounds of falling water are only apparent in early spring.

Negro Creek Trail terminates at the river, where it joins the Sheltowee Trace at a large primitive campsite. While the camping location is perfect, the place can get a little trashed due to heavy use. If you walk upstream a short distance (turning left on the Sheltowee), there is a nice set of bridges that cross Negro Creek. It's worth the slight detour from your loop hike.

Back at the terminus of the Negro Creek and Sheltowee trails, turn right (north) and follow the river downstream. From here, the Sheltowee Trace Trail follows the Big South Fork for 3.1 miles, passing house-sized rocks, multiple creek drainages, and the Cotton Patch Shelter. Just a bit further, on your right, you'll see the remains of an old homestead. A double-hearth, stone fireplace stands firmly aside the trail, amidst stone fences indicating perhaps the family garden or livestock pens. Who were these people and what were they like?

Once you reach Alum Ford, the trail passes through the campground (six primitive sites; $5 per night). Follow the gravel road to KY 700, bear right and up the hill, and you'll immediately see the Sheltowee Trace Trail sign on your left. Duck back into the woods for the last 2 miles of your day. This is a pretty stretch of trail, with more house-sized rocks, two small waterfalls, and lots of towering hemlock and lush rhododendron.

As the trail approaches the Yahoo Falls area, the Sheltowee Trace continues north. Before you climb the stairs to the picnic area, walk just a few more yards down the trail to where the Sheltowee crosses over a small bridge amidst several large rockhouses and a seasonal waterfall high up in the drainage. Turn back around when you're ready and take one step at a time to get to the Yahoo Falls Day Use Area. The trail will pop up around picnic site #15. Turn left to get back to the bathrooms, or wherever you left your vehicle.

Side Trip:
Another nice hike leaves from the Yahoo Falls Day Use Area and takes the Sheltowee Trace north along the South Fork of the Cumberland River. In about two miles you'll reach Big Creek, where the trail continues east for several more miles. Unless you have run shuttle, you will need to retrace your steps back to the parking lot. The web site link below includes a rough map of the area.

Big South Fork National River & Recreation Area
4564 Leatherwood Road
Oneida, TN 37841
Tel: (423) 569-9778
Web: http://goo.gl/RQaidY

Part 2
Urban Walking Trails

This City is what it is because
our citizens are what they are.

~Plato

58 Frankfort: Capitol Grounds Walking Tour

A leisurely walk every Kentuckian should make.

Length: About 1.25 miles
Starting Location: Begin at the large parking lot, due east of the Capitol Annex Building in downtown Frankfort.
Map: http://goo.gl/jUAR5Z

A word or two about maps: A copy of the map with a brief description of all 37 tour sites can be printed off from the web site listed above. Or you can swing by the Frankfort/Franklin County Tourist and Convention Commission office located at 100 Capital Avenue (at the corner of E. Second Street), about five short blocks north of the Capitol building. The tourism office is on the first floor of the ca. 1890s Gooch House, a two and one-half story, frame Queen Anne-style building and the former residence of Rebecca Gooch, of Rebecca-Ruth Candies fame. The office has tons of other brochures available, too. Open Monday-Friday; 8 am–5 pm.

But if you really want to do this walk up right, you should both print out the map *and* get a hard copy of the brochure. Why? Because the two are really quite different and one complements the other. In addition to the printed information, several of the walking tour sites have a prerecorded message that you can listen to by calling (502) 554-9356 and selecting the number of the site posted on the Frankfort PublicArt sign. If you really want to be a geek, you can scan the QR code with your phone. Or, you can simply enjoy the walk and see things for yourself.

So...are the kids off school tomorrow? Friends coming into town this weekend? A mother-in-law you need help with entertaining? Then head to Frankfort and keep everyone busy. Although you could do this walk any day of the year, the best time is spring when all the tulips are trumpeting their colors or mid-summer when the blue salvia is blooming its head off. Fall can also include a nice mum display. And parking is super easy——there are tons of free spots everywhere. Just don't plan on coming when the Legislature is in session or you won't get any work done.

The walking tour takes a winding route all around the Capitol building and the sites range from the large floral clock (loaded with 10,000 flowers and 500-pound (each) minute and hour hands); various tree specimens (including an American chestnut, Kentucky coffee, and a Japanese Zelkova); and the site of two time capsules. Interestingly, the capitol grounds were designed by John Charles Olmsted and Frederick Law Olmsted, Jr., sons of the father of landscape architecture, Frederick Law Olmsted.

For many of you, the highlight might be the capitol building itself, with its Beaux Arts-style of architecture, including elements of classical and Greek architecture, and highly-ornate French styling. Free tours of the building are available by calling (502) 564-3449. The murals on the rotunda, finally completed in 2009 using generous donations, are worth a look inside.

The Governor's Mansion garden was completed during the John Y. Brown administration and is suppose to evoke the feeling of a formal French garden. The Governor's Mansion is also worth an inside tour. Regularly scheduled public tours (also free) are offered every Tuesday and Thursday morning from 9 am–11 am (except for all state and some federal holidays). You can call (502) 564-3449 for more information.

Side Tours:

Before leaving the area you may want to swing by 509 Shelby Street to see the Zeigler House, designed by Frank Lloyd Wright. The private home is about two blocks northeast of the Capitol building and a stone's throw from the walking tour route. See frankfortpublicart.com/sites/zeigler-house for more info.

If you're on a historical roll, drive 5 minutes to Liberty Hall, 202 Wilkinson Street. Guided tours of the house are available for a minimal charge; walking the gardens is free. Call (502) 227-2560 or go to libertyhall.org for tour times. The surrounding streets are pleasant to walk and have some beautiful old homes as well.

Side Detour:

Did all this history leave you hungry? Head over to Rick's White Light Diner, a Frankfort institution. It's short on space, a little lax on cleanliness, but big on flavor. Beignets for breakfast, crawfish pie for lunch, and deep-fried Oreos for dessert. Closed for dinner. Located at 114 Bridge Street, Frankfort, KY 40601. (502) 696-9104. whitelightdiner.com

Frankfort/Franklin County Tourist and Convention Commission
100 Capital Avenue
Frankfort, KY 40601
Phone: (502) 875-8687 or toll free at (800) 960-7200
Web: visitfrankfort.com

59 Frankfort: Downtown Walking Tour

You can eat and drink your way along this one!

Length: About 1.5 miles

Starting Location: Old State Capitol, corner of Broadway and Lewis Streets, Frankfort. Free parking is available in the lot at the rear of the building.

Map: A copy of the map is available from the Frankfort/Franklin County Tourist and Convention Commission office located at 100 Capital Avenue (at the corner of E. Second Street). The tourism office is on the first floor of the ca. 1890s Gooch House, a 2 and one-half story, frame Queen Anne-style building and the former residence of Rebecca Gooch, of Rebecca-Ruth Candies fame. The office has tons of other brochures available, too. Open Monday-Friday 8 am–5 pm. Too bad the map isn't online, but the Gooch house is worth a visit.

The downtown Frankfort walking tour winds its way through a 10-block portion of the city. The walk begins at the Old State Capitol building that was built on the ashes of the two previous capitol buildings and features a self-supporting circular staircase. Kentucky governor William Goebel, after only four days in office, was shot on the grounds and a plaque on the brick walkway marks the spot where he fell. Many Kentuckians did not deem his death a great loss for the Commonwealth. The building is open Tuesday through Saturday, 10 am– 4 pm.

Many private residences, including those of Revolutionary War soldiers, Civil War generals, court justices, governors, senators, and attorneys, populate the tour. Private industry is also represented with various distillers, a cabinetmaker, a musician, and other artists.

Several of these former residents had colorful lives—Amos Kendall, a well-known journalist and tutor to the Henry Clay family, supported Andrew Jackson in his presidential bid against ol' Hank. Later, Amos went on to help establish the School for the Deaf and Mute, now known as Gallaudet College of Washington, DC. Other interesting stories involve the Bibb-Burnley House, at 411 Wapping Street, where John Bibb developed Bibb lettuce. And in 1825, Jero Beauchamp murdered Colonel Solomon P. Sharp in his home. Purportedly this "crime of politics and passion" inspired Robert Penn Warren's novel *World Enough and Time*, as well as another literary effort by Edgar Allen Poe.

Churches are scattered along the walking tour, with careful representation of the mainstream Christian faiths, including Presbyterian, Baptist, Episcopalian, and Catholic. And the Grand Theatre, located at 308 Saint Clair Street, still hosts live performances and classic films. Originally built in 1911 as a vaudeville house, the theatre underwent a significant renovation in 2009.

The downtown Frankfort walking tour also passes though the St. Clair Street (closed to traffic) and Broadway Avenue neighborhood, which houses many of the more interesting Frankfort shops, art galleries, and restaurants. You may want to begin the day at Magee's Bakery, before having lunch at a Serafini's. After you finish your walk, consider culling a few choices from Capital Cellars bourbon list or listen to some live music at the Kentucky Coffeetree Café. downtownfrankfort.com

Side Tour:

Have you ever been to Daniel and Rebecca Boone's grave in the Frankfort Cemetery? The marker sits high on a bluff overlooking the Kentucky River and the State Capitol Building, only a few blocks from downtown Frankfort. As most people believe, Boone died in Missouri at his son's house. However, there is some confusion whether they dug up the "right" body or only some of the "larger" bones of poor Dan'l. Either way, the monument is a nice tribute to the remarkable man in the felt hat and the woman who bore him 10 children, despite his long absences. Frankfort Cemetery, 215 East Main Street, Frankfort, KY 40601. (502) 227-2403. Hours are dawn to dusk.

Frankfort/Franklin County Tourist and Convention Commission
100 Capital Avenue
Frankfort, KY 40601
Phone: (502) 875-8687 or toll free at (800) 960-7200
Web: visitfrankfort.com

60 Georgetown: Walk Through Time

A relaxing stroll along Main Street.

Length: About 2 miles, with additional side trips suggested.

Starting Location: Intersection of West Main and North Water Street, downtown Georgetown.

Map: Call the Georgetown / Scott County Tourism office, phone numbers listed below. They will kindly mail you a copy of their color brochure, straight to your door.

For those who don't remember, Mayberry was a fictional town synonymous with the heartland of America, where no one locks their doors and the town drunk lets himself in and out of his own cell. And we're not talking phones. With its friendly citizens, American values, and classic architecture, Georgetown could easily be Mayberry, USA. So choose a fine day and give yourself plenty of opportunity to lose yourself in time.

Find a place to park on Main or North Water Street, just west of the courthouse, or at Royal Spring Park on South Water Street. Be sure to wear comfortable strolling shoes and allow at least one and one-half hours if you want to see everything. It's important to note that the walking tour brochure does not include much of an overview map—although it's almost impossible to get lost here. However, if you are directionally challenged, you may want to have a map of downtown Georgetown handy or a compass (which many smart phones have).

The tour begins at the historic Scott County Jail, just north of Royal Springs. Actively used from 1892 to 1990, the Romanesque-style jailhouse harbors some wonderful architectural detail and is slowly being converted to an arts and cultural complex. Imagine the host of local characters that might have done time here and then follow the directions to the next stop.

Many of the houses you'll walk past were built in the early to late 19th century, utilizing a variety of architectural styles, including Italianate, Arts and Crafts, Renaissance, and Greek Revival. Take time to peruse the description of each stop along the way to glean stories such as where the first swimming pool was built (and generously filled by the local fire truck); the scandalous common-law marriage that played a role in Grover Cleveland's presidential campaign; and the art of making wax flowers and fruit.

Agrarian endeavors were widely pursued by the early settlers of Georgetown, including thoroughbred and trotting-horse breeders, hemp manufactures, lumber sales, and even bourbon production. But later entrepreneurs developed a variety of

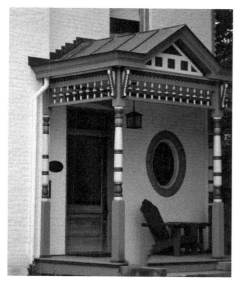

businesses, such as jewelers, confectioners, a Model T Ford dealership, and a progressive factory that manufactured America's first demountable auto wheel.

The Scott County courthouse is an imposing structure, built in the Second Empire Style. Interestingly, the building's Lady of Justice statue does not wear the traditional blindfold over her eyes. Apparently every Halloween Eve she leaves her post and wanders the town looking for injustice that has yet to be punished. You may want to take that into consideration when you plan your foray.

The brochure does include one small typo regarding the unique house located at 416 (and not 414) East Main. The plantation-style house features two separate front porches, a men's smoking and a women's non-smoking. Local legend has it that a ghost, only seen to women, resides at the house. Perhaps it's an apparition of the one woman who defied the smoking rules and ended up on the wrong porch.

On one level, historical walking tours are really just a compilation of stories, as one peels back layers of time. So what will they say about us?

Side Trip:
Royal Springs is stocked with rainbow trout over the months of 6, 7, 8, and 10. Bring your rod and a couple of #16 Adams, #16 BWOs, or a Bead-Head Hare's Ear and you might get lucky.

Georgetown / Scott County Tourism
399 Outlet Center Drive, PO Box 825
Georgetown, KY 40324
Phone: (502) 863-2547 or toll free at (888) 863-8600
Web: georgetownky.com

61 Lexington: African American Heritage Trail

An urban walking trail through downtown Lexington that connects important historical sites of the early African American community.

Length: 3.25 to 4 miles

Starting Location: The starting point for the trail is the Main Street Baptist Church, 582 West Main Street, which is located on the corner of Jefferson and Main, next to the Mary Todd Lincoln House. Parking can be found in the rear or on the street.

Additional Information: You may want to postpone this walk when events are happening at Rupp Arena or the Lexington Convention Center.

Map: http://www.visitlex.com/things-to-do/afam-heritage-trail/

The Project on African American Heritage has greatly benefitted at the local level from Doris Wilkinson, Department of Sociology, University of Kentucky. Part of that effort includes the development of the African American Heritage Trail through downtown Lexington. Maps and brochures can be obtained on-line at the Web address listed above or from the Lexington Convention and Visitors Bureau, at the corner of Rose and Vine streets.

The walking trail takes you to ten different locations of historical significance, beginning at the Main Street Baptist Church. Walking at a brisk pace to all ten sites will easily take you about an hour and a half. A leisurely pace assuring adequate time at each site could take two hours or more. Of course, visiting a smaller combination of sites could result in less time and energy expended.

The trail focuses on sites of African American significance, but the walk takes you through many parts of downtown Lexington, past older homes, interesting shops, renovated office space, restaurants, bars, and the ubiquitous parking lots found in any urban area. Five of the ten sites are churches, with a generous nod to Baptist, Episcopalian, and Christian denominations.

The trail itself requires several street crossings and negotiating uneven sidewalks. However, those with strollers and physical disabilities could easily complete most of the trail. As noted above, it would be important not to attempt this walk any time True Blue Wildcat fans are mobbing Rupp Arena or any famous country music stars are singing in the vicinity. Otherwise, all or parts of the trail could be explored after church on a beautiful Sunday afternoon; before or after dinner at one of downtown Lexington's fine eating establishments; or before a show at the Kentucky Theatre.

Three of the trail's sites are particularly noteworthy to this author. Lexington's very own slave auction block was located at the corner of Cheapside and Main Street (number 3 on the trail map). Cheapside is continuing to serve as a public square and market (but with a much more honorable purpose) with the newly erected Lexington Farmers Market at the same location.

The Historic Pleasant Green Baptist Church, at the corner of West Maxwell and Patterson Streets, claims to be the first black Baptist church west of the Allegheny Mountains (number 4 on the trail map). The Reverend Peter Duerett, a slave of one of Lexington's founding fathers, John Patterson, originally organized the church in 1790 as the African Baptist Church. In 1826, the church's fourth pastor, Reverend George W. Dupee was purchased off the auction block for $850 by a white minister who in turn sold Rev. Dupee back to the congregation in weekly installments, based on Sunday morning offerings.

Although visually cluttered with urban blight, the low area off South Upper Street between Bolivar and Scott Streets (number 5 on the trail map) previously served as a baptismal site for the Historic Pleasant Green Baptist Church. Several black and white photos of well-attended baptisms at this site still exist and allow one to step back in time and feel the water rise above their head. Hallelujah.

Lexington Convention and Visitors Bureau
301 East Vine Street
Lexington, KY 40507
Phone: (859) 233-7299
Web: visitlex.com

Historic Lexington Walking Tours

A series of four walking tours through historic downtown Lexington neighborhoods.

Length: Each self-guided tour is less than 0.5 miles in length

Starting Location: Various downtown locations

Additional Information: The website holds huge pdf files that are painfully slow to download. Beautiful brochures can be picked up from the Blue Grass Trust for Historic Preservation or the Lexington Convention and Visitors Bureau (addresses and numbers listed below). Walks number 58, 59, and 60 are also available as podcasts from the website listed below.

Maps: bluegrasstrust.org/resources.html

The Blue Grass Trust for Historic Preservation has put together four different walking tours of historical homes and other buildings in urban Lexington. None of these are remotely rigorous, unless an image of Confederate General John Hunt Morgan makes your heart race. But you're outside, breathing fresh air, and not sitting at home watching re-runs. Yes, Lexington can be a very interesting place to live.

62 Adaptive Reuse Walking Tour

This tour covers eight buildings along Main Street, running from the old furniture block (now blandly known as The Square) to the Wolf Wile Building (now

Gray Construction). Three other urban neighborhoods are on the tour, including South Hill, Old Vine and North Limestone. For those interested in historic preservation, urban revitalization, architecture, or simply keeping downtown Lexington alive, this one's for you.

A local company, outrageGIS mapping, produced a great map of this walking tour. Try their website to download this one: outrageGIS.com/sample/Lexington-Walking-Tour.pdf

63 Constitution Historic District, between North Limestone Street & North Martin Luther Boulevard, and East Third & Constitution Streets

This tour includes some of today's well-known entities such as Sayre School; the Matthew Kennedy House (now houses the upscale shop Mulberry and Lime); and an 1838-1840 residence (now occupied by Third Street Stuff).

64 Mulberry Hill (renamed North Limestone Street in 1887), between Salem Alley and East Fifth Street

Mulberry Hill was one of two major streets when the city of Lexington was first platted in 1781 (the other being Main Cross Street, later renamed Broadway). The original residents included early millionaires, mayors, congressmen, attorneys, craftsmen, and one of the city's first African American ministers. Architecture runs from Italianate to Greek Revival to simple pyramidal-roof cottages.

65 Gratz Park, bounded by Church and West Third Streets, and North Mill and Market Streets

Gratz Park provides the perfect heart of urban green space for the surrounding historical homes, the Carnegie Center for Literacy and Learning, and Transylvania University. Be sure to see the Patterson log cabin ("Lexington's first mobile home"), the Three Sisters, and The Fountain of Youth.

Blue Grass Trust for Historic Preservation
253 Market Street
Lexington, KY 40507
Phone: (859) 253-0362
Web: bluegrasstrust.org

Lexington Convention and Visitors Bureau
301 East Vine Street
Lexington, KY 40507
Phone: (859) 233-7299
Web: visitlex.com

66 The Lexington Walk

An urban stroll featuring 33 different points of interest in downtown Lexington.

Length: 2 miles

Starting Location: Tour begins at Triangle Park, at the intersection of North Broadway and Main Street.

Map: This walking tour is not available for Internet download. Your best option is to call the Lexington Visitors Center (they will mail you one), or stop by and pick up a map. The map is nicely done, large scale, and informative. The brochure also includes several driving tours and ideas for side trips within the city and the countryside. And it's free.

The Lexington Walk is a combination of new and old locations across the city. It's a great way to familiarize yourself with downtown, including historical sites, the arts, the commercial district, and so forth. It also makes a perfect adjunct to an evening of dining out in one of the city's great urban restaurants or catching a show at the Kentucky Theatre. We also think it's an awesome cheap date or something to do when you have out of town guests. Downtown Lexington is a happening place!

Lexington Convention and Visitors Bureau
401 West Main Street Ste. 104
Lexington, KY 40507
Phone: (800) 845-3959
Web: visitlex.com

67 LexWalk Audio Tour

Grab your smart phone or MP3 player, and groove to an urban Lexington walk-about.

Length: less than 2 miles
Starting Location: Tour starts at Triangle Park, corner of Main Street and Broadway.

Additional Information: This one really brings the geek out in you. Rush hour can be a bit noisy.

Map: http://goo.gl/o5Y4bA
Audio Downloads: http://goo.gl/XLhjbI

This walk is a bit weird as the technology is still trying to catch up with our imaginations. Using your cell phone you can dial a number (859.963.3649) and listen to various points of interest in downtown Lexington. Or, using your smart phone, you can hear the tour and see images by linking to http://myoncell. mobi/18599633649. Alternately, you can download a MP3 version to your player or iPhone using the link provided above. Finally, a free app is also available from the iTunes store.

Choose your technology and start walking. The tour covers 19 points of interest in urban Lexington including historical homes and churches, Transylvania University, and Gratz Park. Move at your own pace. Sit on a bench. People watch. You walk to your own drummer.

Be wary because this type of tour really sucks the memory from a smart phone (unless you use the app version). And the GPS reception is a bit iffy once in the shadows of tall buildings. But, it's free. It's novel. And one day it might be yesterday's latest fad.

**Lexington Convention
and Visitors Bureau**
401 West Main Street Ste. 104
Lexington, KY 40507
**Phone: (800) 845-3959
Web: visitlex.com**

68 Lincoln's Lexington Walking Tour

A combination of Abe and Mary Todd historical sites, integrated with the story of African American life in early Lexington.

Length: 2.5 miles

Starting Location: Walk begins at Phoenix Park, adjacent to the downtown Lexington Public Library, at the corner of Limestone and Main Streets.

Additional Information: The map is available for download as a .pdf file but takes forever. You may prefer to just pick one up at the Mary Todd Lincoln House or at the downtown Lexington Public Library.

Brochure and Map: mtlhouse.org/documents/WalkingTour.pdf

For Lincoln fans this is a must-do walk. The brochure is filled with information —all in print so big you may be able to leave your reading glasses at home. Of course, starting with a tour of the Mary Todd Lincoln house and museum might be the ideal way to begin. The museum also has a self-guided walking tour brochure of the Lexington Cemetery (also free for download or obtained at the house).

Mary Todd Lincoln House
578 West Main Street
Lexington, KY 40507
Phone: (859) 233-9999
Web: mtlhouse.org

69 Legacy Trail

A 12-foot wide, 12-mile long paved, multi-use interpretive trail and developing public art venue that connects urban Lexington with the Kentucky Horse Park.

Length: 1 to 17 miles
Map: mylegacytrail.com
Directions: The Legacy Trail can be reached via five different trailheads:

TH1. Isaac Murphy Memorial Art Garden Trailhead, corner of East Third Street and Midland Avenue. The 3.5-mile section of the trail between the trailhead and the Northside YMCA trailhead simply follows downtown Lexington streets. There are no dedicated hiking or biking lanes on this section, so you're on your own.

TH2. Northside YMCA Trailhead, adjacent to the North Lexington Family YMCA, 381 West Loudon Ave.

TH3. Coldstream Trailhead #1. From downtown Lexington travel north on Newtown Pike, left on Citation Boulevard, and right on McGrathiana Parkway until you see the signs.

TH4. Coldstream Trailhead #2. From downtown Lexington travel north on Newtown Pike, left on Aristides Boulevard, right on McGrathiana Parkway, and right on Coldstream A, until you see the signs.

TH5. North Legacy Trailhead, off Berea Road and directly across from the Kentucky Horse Park Campground on Iron Works Pike.

Additional Information: Permitted uses include biking, walking, skating, jogging, and strollers. No motorized vehicles or horses. Remember to keep to the right and pass on the left, and move off the trail when stopped. No drinking water is available along the trail. Pets must be leashed and owners must remove all waste.

The Legacy Trail is a multi-use trail with urban Lexington as one bookend and the Kentucky Horse Park as the other. In between, the trail meanders through downtown Lexington, the Lexmark campus, Coldstream Research Park, and part of the University of Kentucky's Agricultural Research Station (including Coldstream, Maine Chance, and Spindletop Farms).

Phase One of the trail, covering approximately 8.5 miles one-way, opened in September 2010, and runs between the Northside YMCA and the Kentucky Horse Park. Phase Two will include the completion of the Isaac Murphy Memorial Art Garden, and will run along Third and Jefferson Streets, until reaching Loudon Avenue to connect with the Northside YMCA Trailhead.

The Phase One trail is paved asphalt, with the exception of one mile of permeable concrete at the Coldstream Trailhead (rendering that section quite the bumpy ride for in-line skaters). Evolving landscaping will include native grasses, shrubs, and trees; more public art; benches; and hopefully at least one water spigot. Several interpretive signs refer to Cane Branch, which parallels the trail in several places.

The trail passes over several nicely designed bridges, one underpass, and one tunnel (getting you from one side of I-75 to the other). The only busy street crossing is at the corner of Newtown Pike and Citation Boulevard (at a crosswalk). In general the trail is flat to gently rolling, although the exposed countryside can leave the trail user vulnerable to gusting winds.

The Phase Two trail begins at the Isaac Murphy Memorial Art Garden and runs west along East Third Street (again, note that there is not a dedicated hiking or biking lane); makes a loop along North Upper Street, to Main Street, and then back along North Limestone; continues along Third Street until north on Jefferson;

and finally left on Loudon Avenue until you get to the Northside YMCA. If reading this makes you dizzy, it might be best to take a copy of the map with you. Quite honestly, if you want to walk the streets of urban Lexington, we suggest making another selection from this book.

Eventually the trail is slated to connect with other trail systems throughout Central Kentucky. But for now, this is a wonderful addition to those wanting to get outdoors and get some exercise.

Far Side Trip:
If you like this type of trail, another option might be the Berea Bike Path, which is approximately 2.3 miles one-way. This paved trail runs from the Kentucky Artisan Center (located off I-75, at exit #77) to downtown Berea. From Lexington it's a 40-minute drive for a short trail, but it might be a nice alternative for runners, young bikers or the stroller set. Of course, finding a small café in Berea or browsing the local craft markets might round out the day.

Versailles also has a nice paved trail, suitable for walking and riding. A map can be found at: http://goo.gl/MqfVIR

70 Shared Use and Other Paved Trails in Lexington

Many short, paved trails are scattered across Lexington, located in both the city's larger parks as well as many smaller neighborhood parks.

Length: 0.5 to 2.5+ miles
Location: varies
Additional Information: Be sure to understand the distinction between a shared use trail and a walking trail, as described below. Water and trash receptacles are rarely available.

Web: lexingtonky.gov/index.aspx?page=262

Over 50 paved trailettes exist in parks throughout Fayette County and the number is growing all the time. Lexington does a good job maintaining these pathways. A current and complete list can be found at the web address above.

These trails are great for younger children, the mobility-challenged, and harried workers needing a quick respite from the stresses of the day. Permitted uses include walking, biking, skating, and running. The trails are also suitable for strollers. The accompanying green space allows for pockets of urban woods and meadows, accommodating a variety of urban-tolerant flora and fauna.

The city has two primary classifications for paved trails. The following description is taken verbatim from the website listed above:

A **SHARED USE TRAIL** is paved and designed for activities such as running and walking, as well as higher speed activities like bicycling and skating. They are 10 to 12 feet wide.

A **WALKING TRAIL** is paved and at least 8 feet wide. For everyone's safety, bicycling and skating at greater than a fast walking speed is not allowed on walking trails.

The following list is a subset of the longer trails that have been developed. (Only paved trails a half-mile or longer in length have been included.) Distances are one-way.

Park	Length in Miles	Trail Information
Arboretum Trail	2.0	Walking trail off Alumni Dr.; No bikes allowed.
Beaumont Preserve	0.9	Walking trail spur off Cardinal Run Park Trail; Access behind Rosa Parks Elementary School; naturalized area
Brighton Rail Trail	1.84	Shared use trail from Man O' War Blvd. to Pleasant Ridge Park and Polo Club Blvd.
Cardinal Run South Park	1.2	Shared use trail off Parkers Mill Rd.
Coldstream Park	1.2	Shared use trail spur off Legacy Trail located off McGrathiana Pkwy
Constitution	0.9	Walking trail off Old Paris Pike/Rookwood
Day Treatment Center Trail	0.6	Walking trail off Red Mile Place (connects to Addison Park)
Dogwood Trace Park	0.6	Walking trail off Dogwood Trace Blvd.
Gainesway Park	0.6	Walking trail off Appian Way
Garden Springs Park	0.5	Walking trail off Garden Springs Park
Gleneagles Greenway	0.7	Unpaved path off of Polo Club Blvd in greenway with native planting
Harrod Hill Park	0.5	Walking trail off Ridgecane Rd.
Hartland Park	0.5	Walking trail off Kenesaw Rd.
Higbee Mill Park	0.5	Walking trail off corner of Claysmill Rd. and Old Higbee Mill Rd.
Kirklevington Park	0.9	Walking trail off Redding Rd.
Lakeview Park	0.5	Walking trail off Laketower Dr.
Lansdowne-Merrick Park	1.4	Walking trail/path off Pepperhill Rd. beside Julius Marks Elementary School
Legacy Trail	1 to 17	Shared use trail. (See entry #65)
Liberty Park Trail	1.3	Shared use trail off Starshoot Pkwy.
Martin Luther King Park	1.2	Walking trail off McCullough Dr.
Riverhill Park	0.5	Walking trail and sidewalk
Shillito Park/Lafayette Trail	2.5	1.5 mile shared use trail loop; connects to 1.0 mile of Lafayette shared use trail

Park	Length in Miles	Trail Information
South Elkhorn	0.5	Walking trail off Newbury Way
Southpoint Park	0.5	Walking trail off Graves Dr.
Squires Road Trail	1.3	Shared use trail from Summerhill Dr. to Squires Rd.; access at Berry Hill Park
Town Branch Trail	1.9	Shared use trail off Long Branch Ln. across from Masterson Station Park
Valley Park	0.5	Walking trail and path off Cambridge Dr.
Veterans Park	1.4	Walking trail off Southpoint Dr.
Waverly Park	0.7	Walking trail off Twain Ridge Rd.
Wellington Park	1.5	Walking trail off Wellington Way
Wellington Trail	1.5	Shared use trail along Keithshire Way/Reynolds Rd.; connects to Shillito Park/Lafayette Trail

71 Richmond: Historical and Architectural Walking Tour

For both the casual stroller and the serious lover of architecture.

Length: About 2 miles
Starting Location: Richmond KY Tourism, 345 Lancaster Avenue

Map: This one is not available for download and must be picked up directly from the Richmond KY Tourism office (listed below). The current walking tour "brochure" weighs in at a full 77 pages, describing 60 historical homes and commercial buildings, plus 6 more properties in the appendix that aren't quite walking distance. You may want to call ahead to be sure that they still have some in stock, because the brochure/booklet really is an essential part of the tour. Also be sure to pick up the other brochure that enables you to take a free self-guided tour of "Irvinton", the house where the tourism office resides.

Built in 1820, Irvinton served as a private home for many years, before being converted to a Trachoma Hospital (you may have to look that one up!) Eventually the house was deeded over to the city of Richmond. The home is beautifully furnished with period antiques, many of which belonged to previous homeowners; an authentic Revolutionary War uniform (one of only seven remaining); a wreath made entirely out of human hair (yes, a lost art); and several period dresses and men's jackets. And the Sine Pendulum located in the gun room is guaranteed to tempt you to try it *just once*.

After you've resisted all temptation to try the pendulum, head out the door with the walking tour booklet in hand. Basically you'll want to head northeast along Lancaster Avenue, towards Main Street. While most buildings are lined along East and West Main Street, there are a few scattered along Second, Third, and Water Streets.

If you stop in front of each building, read each entry, and observe every architectural detail, darkness will surely fall upon you. But some of the details are quite interesting and the stories evoked could fill an Oprah best seller.

Many of you reading this are familiar with the Federal and Italianate styles of architecture, dogtrots, gable roofs, sidelights, fanlights, and so forth. But do you know what bracketed window hoods are? Fluted pilasters? Or the difference between smooth and rusticated ashlar-cut stone? Enjoy the walk and add these terms and more to your vocabulary.

But history is also stories and vignettes. Why were men only permitted to use the front entrance at Glyndon's Hotel? Why did women have to use a separate side entrance? And why did Daniel's brother carve "1770 Squire Boone" into a large boulder that now sits inside the courthouse? And how cool would it be if horse-drawn trolleys still ran down Main Street?

Side Trip:
For a real treat, stop by Purdy's Coffee, 212 West Main, for a cup of Peruvian Cococho and a delectable pastry. Breakfast and lunch served all day. Closed Sundays.

Richmond KY Tourism
345 Lancaster Avenue
Richmond, KY 40475
Phone: (859) 626-8474 or toll free at (800) 866-3705
Web: richmondkytourism.com

72 Winchester: Downtown Walking Tour

History and folklore serve as the mortar that holds these brick and stone buildings together.

Length: Approximately 1.5 miles.
Starting Location: Corner of Main and Broadway, Kerr Building, Winchester

Map: You can download and print a nice brochure at http://goo.gl/CERfYT, or just pull it up on your smart phone as you walk along.

The walking tour starts at the corner of North Main Street and West Broadway, and begins with one of the most vivid stories found along the way. If you crane your neck and look at the top of the old Kerr Building, ca 1889, you'll see a proud rooster calmly surveying his domain. Story has it that two local businessmen were debating the outcome of the 1932 presidential election between Franklin D. Roosevelt and Herbert Hoover. Given that times were tough and money was tight, the bet included wagers of the loser pushing a peanut up Main Street with his nose, versus standing atop the Kerr Building and flapping one's arms and crowing. As history unfolded, Roosevelt won and the stories continue.

Across North Main Street from the Kerr Building is the birthplace of Helen Thomas, the well-known United Press White House correspondent who made famous the phrase "Thank you, Mr. President", used when beginning and ending press conferences. Undoubtedly, Ms. Thomas must have frequented Leeds Theatre, just a half-block up Main Street. Walking another block north, you'll see the now-empty Sphar & Company feed store, used as a back-drop for two movies——*The Flimflam Man* and *Black Beauty*.

Heading south on Main Street brings you to the Clark County Courthouse, with its 1907 clocktower still intact. Apparently pigeons also had a liking for the clock face, as evidenced by their propensity for roosting on the minute hand. Despite the caretaker's diligent efforts to shoo the pigeons off, the clock frequently ran 15 minutes late. Maybe life in small town America really does slow down.

Across Court Street is the Citizen's National Bank, circa 1886-1889, showcasing rusticated stonework, elaborate gables, and beautiful ironwork. Predominate to the front entrance are two carved medallion faces of Lizzie Winn and Mary Miller, daughters of the two founders of the bank.

Downtown Winchester is similar to many other towns of its size, alternating pawnshops with attorney offices, majestic churches with stately homes, and social service offices with apartment buildings. Winchester is struggling to preserve and celebrate its rich heritage of people and events. Fortunately, the town has many people who care and work tirelessly to collect every story and renovate every building worth saving.

Side Trips:
You may want to link your historical walking tour of Winchester with the Bluegrass Heritage Museum, located at 217 South Main Street, in the 1887 Ishmael house. (859) 745-1358. bgheritage.com

If you're hungry, check out the Engine House Deli, located in the 1886 fire station at 9 West Lexington Ave. (859) 737-0560.

Or try Graze Market and Café, for an authenticate field to table experience, found at 150 Combs Ferry Road, Winchester, KY 40351. (859) 745-0990. grazelex.com.

Winchester-Clark County Tourism Commission
2 S. Maple Street
Winchester, KY 40391
Phone: (859) 744-0556 or toll free at (800) 298-9105
Web: www.TourWinchester.com

Part 3
Gardens

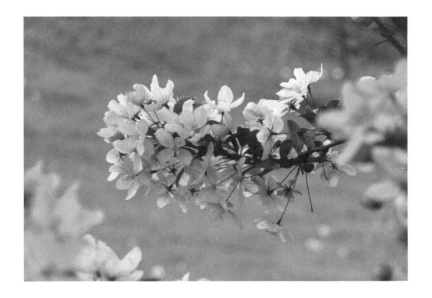

Gardens... should be like lovely, well-shaped girls:

all curves, secret corners,

unexpected deviations, seductive surprises

and then still more curves.

~H.E. Bates, A Love of Flowers

73 The Arboretum: State Botanical Garden of KY

One hundred acres of gardens, green space, and walking paths.

Length: 0.25 to 2 miles of paved trail, plus multiple interconnecting gravel trails and dirt paths

Facilities: Visitor center; bathrooms and water available when open.

Hours: Open 365 days a year. The gardens are open from dawn until dusk daily. The visitor center is open Monday–Friday, 8:30 am-4 pm. See web site for Kentucky Children's Garden fees and hours. Docent-led tours are also available. Closed during UK home football games.

Additional Information: Permitted uses include walking, jogging, and picnicking. Walkers have the right-of-way on the trails. No bicycles, except for transportation to and from the arboretum. Dog are permitted on paved trails only and must be leashed. No specimen collecting.

Directions: 500 Alumni Drive, between Tates Creek and Nicholasville Roads (just south of the University of Kentucky football stadium), Lexington.

The 100-acre arboretum ranges from formal gardens to paved trails to a small urban wood loaded with chattering squirrels and invasive honeysuckle. Easily reached by car or bike, the gardens are a joint venture between the University of Kentucky and the Lexington-Fayette Urban County Government.

From the parking area you will be able to see the Dorothea Smith Oatts Visitation Center and the start of the developed garden areas including rose, herb, and vegetable gardens; the All-American trials and displays; home fruit and nut plantings; and a variety of hardscapes (gazebos, pergolas, stone fences, ponds, and more).

The 2-mile paved trail wraps around the perimeter of the park, and is a popular place for walkers, joggers, and baby strollers. Various spurs off the main trail also showcase the seven geophysical regions of Kentucky. An additional one-half mile trail wanders through the arboretum woods. A nice map of the area is available from their website.

The Kentucky Children's Garden targets the two to ten year-old crowd. Covering nearly two acres, this area includes child-scaled theme gardens and a small amphitheater. The Arboretum's Little Sprouts program is also quite popular. Although there is no admission fee for the general gardens, unfortunately there are fees for the Children's Garden. Please see the website for the fee scale and posted hours which vary throughout the year.

Also visit the website for upcoming events. Past activities have been as diverse as a scarecrow parade, bonsai exhibit, flower-arranging classes, and a riparian buffer restoration workshop.

The Arboretum, State Botanical Garden of Kentucky
500 Alumni Drive
Lexington, KY 40503
Phone: (859) 257-6955
Web: http://arboretum.ca.uky.edu

74 Ashland: The Henry Clay Estate

Sitting on the original outskirts of Lexington, Hank's house provides an urban oasis of mature trees and a formal boxwood garden.

Facilities: Historical home tours and outdoor café (in season). Bathrooms and water available during tour hours.

Hours: The grounds are open year round, sunrise to sunset. The formal garden is open when the house is open for tours: Tuesday–Saturday, 10 am–4 pm; and Sunday 1 pm–4 pm. Closed Mondays, major holidays, and the month of January, with limited access in February.

Additional Information: Sorry, no picnicking except for special events.

Directions: Heading out of downtown Lexington, East Main becomes Richmond Road. Soon after the tree-lined boulevard forms, take a right on Sycamore. If you miss the house, go back home.

Most people know of Henry Clay as the "Great Compromiser" who served multiple terms in both the US Senate and the House of Representatives, and as Secretary of State. Fewer Lexitonians know that Clay is also credited with introducing Hereford cattle to the US and the mint julep to Washington, or that he was the first to lie in state at the US Capitol. Sadly, seven of Clay's 11 children preceded him in death. Clay's will contained lengthy provisions for his slaves, including educational opportunities and a time frame for their release to freedom.

Ashland, the home of Henry and Lucretia Hart Clay, was razed after his death. The house had fallen into disrepair, in part because of faulty mortar used in the brick home. Clay's son, James, rebuilt the house on the same foundation, using the original floor plan and salvaged building materials from the original house. Although the land the house sits on is only a fraction of the original estate, the property has retained its stately air in a gracious nod to its first owner.

This entry did not make the book for its heart-pumping trails. But don't overlook its cardio benefits either. Ashland makes for a perfect biking destination or a quiet stroll to shake off the stressors of the day. A wood chip path winds its way across the property, past the historic home, and through the peony and boxwood gardens. While not paved, the walking paths are quite level. Add a relaxing lunch at the Gingko Tree café (located on the brick patio around the old smokehouse) or a tour of the home, and your blood pressure will drop ten points.

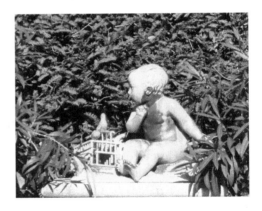

Ashland: The Henry Clay Estate
120 Sycamore Road
Lexington, KY 40502
Phone: (859) 266-8581
Web: henryclay.org

75 Jack Jouett House Historic Site

Historical home, native tree walk, colonial herb garden, and fruitery, all neatly packaged on five acres.

Facilities: Small visitor center, restrooms. Free tours of the buildings.

Hours: Open April through October: Monday 10 am-noon; Friday noon-5 pm; Saturday 10 am-5 pm; Sunday 1-5 pm. Tours also available by appointment throughout the year.

Directions: Definitely not an "urban" garden, but it's not far from town. From Lexington, head out Versailles Road (US 60 W) for the Bluegrass Parkway. Take the first exit, #68 on the BG Parkway, for Versailles. Turn right (north) onto KY 33. Drive 0.4 miles. Turn left onto KY 2113, aka Falling Springs Boulevard. Drive 1.2 miles. Turn left onto KY 1964, McCowan's Ferry Road. Drive south for 4.3 miles. Turn right (west) on Craig's Creek Road. The Jouett House is 0.2 miles on your left.

The Executive Director of the Jouett House has a vision. A long-term vision. The newly planted Native Tree Walk is comprised of 39 different specimens, some no taller than a toddler, including pignut hickory, Kentucky coffee tree, persimmon, sassafras, and witch hazel to name a few. Upon arriving at the Jouett House, head downhill to the visitor center to pick up a nice walking guide of the site. There is also a four-page densely-packed companion piece describing each species in detail. Who knew that beech is part of the oak family and that persimmon wood was used to make golf clubs? Thank you Bill Fountain for putting this together.

The historical site offers an herb garden, with over 20 herbs, including chamomile, feverfew, tansy, and pennyroyal, all harking of the past. Herbs were an essential part of pioneer life as they were used for flavoring and preserving foods and for medicinal purposes. Again there is a four-page, densely-packed companion piece describing each herb in detail. For all this we can be grateful to the Woodford Herbalists Club.

Finally, there is a newly-planted fruitery, with promises of currants, fresh figs, black raspberries, peaches, and apples ripening throughout the seasons. Again, most of the specimens are young, but the local deer population is patiently waiting.

While you won't get much exercise walking the grounds, your mind will have plenty of room to roam when listening to the stories of how Jack Jouett became the "Paul Revere of the South". Together, Jack and Sally Jouett expanded the original one-room stone house and loft with a two-story, five-room brick home, connected with a dogtrot. The house is incredibly well preserved and fortunate to have so many dedicated people preserving its future.

Side Trip:
While in the Versailles vicinity, you might want to stop by the Heike Pickett Gallery & Sculpture Garden, located in the historic Carter House, built in 1792. It's less than a ten-minute drive from the Jouett House. The Gallery is open free to the public at 110 Morgan Street, Versailles, KY 40383. Hours: 11 am-4 pm, Thursday through Saturday, or by appointment. (859) 233-1263. www.heikepickettgallery.com

Jack Jouett House Historic Site
255 Craig's Creek Road
Versailles, KY 40383
Phone: (859) 873-7902
Web: www.Jouetthouse.org

76 Josephine Sculpture Park

A sculpture garden and growing vision of how to integrate art into the natural world around us.

Facilities: Small visitor center and even smaller restrooms.

Hours: Daily, dawn to dusk.

Directions: Take exit #53A off I-64, just south of Frankfort. Head south on US Hwy 127 towards Lawrenceburg. Drive about 0.8 miles. Turn left (east) on KY 420N. Drive 0.1 miles. Turn right (south) at the four-way stop onto Lawrenceburg Road. Drive another 0.9 miles and the park will be on your right.

The Josephine Sculpture Park is an interesting place to wander across open meadows, while discovering more than 35 large sculptures and graffiti-style murals. Covering 20 acres of retired farmland, the park is a maze of mowed paths that in the summertime meander through Queen Anne's lace, butterfly weed, vetch, teasel, thistle, and chicory. However, if sculpture is not your thing, you may want to make another choice, as the art is the primary focus.

While several of the sculptures were made by Kentucky artists, many of the contributors are scattered across the United States from Minnesota to California. The materials also vary from chainsaw wood and metal sculptures to whimsically-painted wood and cast concrete. Most sculptures are nicely labeled with a little background information about the sculptor, a brief artist statement, and helpful notes as to whether the works can be respectfully touched or climbed upon.

Some of the sculptures can be downright quirky, such as the Tractor Town Titan who would have been best buds with Lighting McQueen and Mator if he lived closer to Radiator Springs. But other sculptures can be downright biting in their political wit such as the Scarecrow from the Industrial Farm, who hangs in mourning beneath the eaves of an old barn.

The Josephine Sculpture Park also hosts several community performance art events each year. Check out their web page for more information.

A Far-Far-Side Trip:

If you find outdoor sculpture intriguing, seriously consider a road trip to Sisters of Loretto Motherhouse, south of Bardstown. The work of Jeanne Dueber is on display both inside the gallery and scattered across the nearby fields. Dueber is known for her works, which explore the interactions between spirituality, faith, and the human figure. Sisters of Loretto, 515 Nerinx Road, Nerinx, KY 40049. (270) 865-5811. http://goo.gl/6owfNK

The Josephine Sculpture Park
3355 Lawrenceburg Road
Frankfort, KY 40601
Phone: (502) 352-7082
Web: josephinesculpturepark.org/

77 Lexington Cemetery

Over 170 acres of floral displays, native tree species, fountains, and koi ponds, keeping company those who have been laid to rest.

Facilities: None, although the office may be an option for emergencies.

Hours: Open 365 days a year. Visiting is permitted daily 8 am–5 pm. The office is open weekdays 8 am–4 pm, and Saturday 8 am–noon.

Additional Information: Please be quiet and respectful. This is not a public park. No picnicking or rowdy kids. Bikes and motorcycles can be parked at the front entrance. All pets must be on leash.

Directions: Head out of downtown Lexington, on W. Main Street. Just past Newtown Pike, cross over the bridge and you will see the large stone entrance to the cemetery on your right.

Established in 1849, Lexington Cemetery has some of the oldest trees and tombstones in the area. Over 200 species of trees can be found, with the arboretum tour identifying 41 of those with metal plates. The dogwoods and pink weeping cherries are spectacular in the spring, with ginkgos and sassafras providing fall color, and shellbark hickories for winter interest.

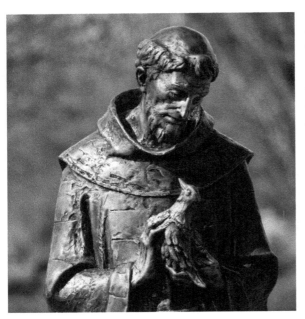

For history buffs, a stroll through the grounds will bring you to the graves of such Lexington notables as Henry Clay, General John Hunt Morgan, and Coach Adolph Rupp. In addition, more than 500 Confederate and 1,100 Union veterans are buried here.

The Lexington Cemetery website includes a map of the area, a tree guide, and a bird checklist. The office can also provide information on activities with children and a history of Lexington in the cemetery.

Side Trip:
If you enjoy the peace of strolling though cemeteries, upon leaving Lexington Cemetery turn right on West Main. Very shortly, turn left at 874 West Main and drive through the gates of Calvary Cemetery, Lexington's final resting place for those of Catholic faith. Owned by the Catholic Diocese Of Lexington, a quiet stroll will find you at the far end of the cemetery, and the Ava Maria and Priests sections.

Lexington Cemetery
833 West Main Street
Lexington, KY 40508
Phone: (859) 255-5522
Web: www.lexcem.org

78 Nannine Clay Wallis Arboretum

A small urban garden, adjacent to the historical Wallis House, and home to the Garden Club of Kentucky.

Facilities: None

Hours: Daily, sunrise to sunset

Additional Information: The house and grounds are available for rental. For guided tours and a copy of their extensive study guide, call the number below.

Directions: From Lexington, take North Broadway towards Paris (which becomes Paris Pike). From where North Broadway crosses under I-75, drive approximately 14.5 miles to Paris, KY. Turn right on 7th Street and drive one short city block. Just past Pleasant Street, you'll see a small parking lot on your left, adjacent to the gardens. Park here.

Nannine Clay Wallis was one of the original founders of the Garden Club of Kentucky and went on to become both its president and that of The National Council of State Garden Clubs. Upon her death in 1970, Mrs. Wallis donated the house and gardens for horticultural preservation and educational programs.

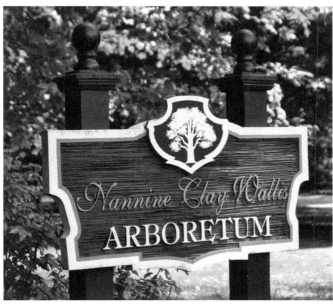

Although small in size for an arboretum, the gardens are known for their old tree collection, many of which were planted in the mid-1850s. At that time, planting the newest species of tree or flower was somewhat of a status symbol and an indication of the owner being both well-to-do and well-traveled. A study guide is available from the Garden Club.

Side Trip:
While in Paris, you may want to stroll the streets of downtown. The town of Paris hosts several ArtWalks throughout the year in which artists set up outdoor stands and local galleries and museums are open in the evening. You can check pariskytourism.com for a current calendar of events.

Nannine Clay Wallis Arboretum
616 Pleasant Street
Paris, KY 40361
Phone: 859-987-6158
Web: http://www.gardenclubky.org/arboretum/

79 Scott County Native Plants Arboretum

Located on the campus of Georgetown College, a very small collection of native Kentucky flora.

Facilities: None. However bathrooms and water may be available inside various college buildings.

Hours: None posted

Directions: From Lexington, head north on Georgetown Street (US 25), which later becomes Lexington Road and then Broadway Street. At the Georgetown courthouse, turn right (east) on Main Street. Park where you can.

After finding a place to park, stroll down the heart of Georgetown, window-shopping as you go and marveling how small town America can continue to thrive in the realm of Wally World and box stores. Promise yourself to support the local merchants.

Eventually walk far enough east on Main Street, to the corner of Memorial Drive (three short blocks from the courthouse). Behind the W. Morgan Patterson

House you'll find the Scott County Native Plants Arboretum, which was established in the mid-1990s.

The arboretum is small (less than one-half acre in size), and showcases trees, woody plants, and herbaceous perennials native to Kentucky. The Woodland Garden brings you ferns and wild ginger; the Prairie Garden includes coneflowers and mints; and in the Native Grass Garden you'll find bluestem, goldenrod, and asters. Several woody species are easily identified (and if you need help, signs are posted), including witch hazel, paw paw, downy serviceberry, fringe tree, and spice and buttonbushes. With the growing emphasis on the need to plant more native species in our urban environments, it's fun to see these guys in action.

In the middle of the arboretum hangs the first of ten public sculptures scattered throughout the Georgetown College campus. Maps are available on-site showing the location of each sculpture and a short description of the piece. And that's a good thing if you have trouble interpreting modern art. But walking the collection provides additional visual interest as you explore parts of Georgetown's campus.

Side Trip:

Before returning to your vehicle, stop at Fava's (159 East Main Street) for a bit of lunch or early dinner. Established in 1910, Fava's has been described as an "amazing old-fashioned diner without hype or kitsch." The hand-painted mural on the wall is quite fun.

Scott County Native Plants Arboretum
Corner of E. Main Street and Memorial Drive
Georgetown, KY 40324

80 Waveland State Historic Site

As part of the Kentucky park system, visitors are free to walk the grounds of this mid-nineteenth century Greek revival plantation.

Facilities: Playground equipment, picnic tables, historical home tours, and a kid-sized log cabin. Bathrooms and water available during tours.

Hours: Daily, sunrise to sunset. See the website for the home tour hours.

Directions: From the intersection of Nicholasville Road and Man O' War Boulevard, travel south a scant 0.5 mile. Turn right on Waveland Museum Lane, then right again into the park.

Don't be misled by the historic designation——although the ties to Daniel Boone, beautiful architecture, and period furnishings might be enough to draw you on a tour of the home. However, the grounds are free to roam and perfect for the rug rat set. It is on the small side, even for an urban park, but can fill a large niche in a child's heart.

In sight from the parking lot are several picnic tables and playground equipment, making this a popular spot for birthday parties on weekends. A very miniature log cabin, complete with real wooden mantle and stone chimney, is a delight for hobbits and small earthlings alike. Let the kids and grandkids burn off their energy by running along the short nature trail at the wood's edge and racing over the small wooden bridges.

The older folks can take in the small flower and herb gardens, or admire the stone, brick, and log construction of the slave quarters, icehouse, and smokehouse. Sometimes we all yearn for a simpler way of life.

Waveland State Historic Site
225 Waveland Museum Lane
Lexington, KY 40514
Phone: (859) 272-3611
Web: http://parks.ky.gov/parks/historicsites/waveland/

81 Woodland Park Tree Trail

A great way to test your tree identification skills any time of the year.

Facilities: Restrooms, drinking water, pool (all seasonal); ball courts; ball field; skate park; playground; picnic tables and shelter; and open areas for the jugglers and tai chi practitioners who like to congregate here. Pets on leash are permitted.

Hours: None posted.

Directions: Located in urban Lexington, bounded by High Street, Kentucky Avenue, and Clay Avenue (but not Woodland Avenue!)

Most Lexitonians have been to Woodland Park one time or another—picked up a game of tennis, hung out at the skate park, strolled the Woodland Art Fair or watched the kids play beneath the pirate ship paradoxically stranded in the middle of the urban pool. But did you know that there's a tree trail here, too?

Before leaving the house print out the brochure cited below or, being more tree-friendly, simply pull it up on your smart phone. Forty-seven trees are clearly marked with a plaque embedded in the ground underneath each tree. The brochure helps you sort out the Quercus pagoda from the Quercus Montana, and the text includes little interesting snippets about each variety. From the Kentucky coffee tree to the persimmon and bald cypress, many native trees can be found in the park. But a few oddballs are thrown in here, such as the weeping Alaskan-cedar and the Chinese elm, also native, but just not to Kentucky.

There are many people to acknowledge and organizations to thank for creating the tree trail. Their efforts are greatly appreciated.

Web: www2.ca.uky. edu/forestry/ Woodland.pdf

82 Yuko-En on the Elkhorn and the Cardome Walking Trail

A friendship garden integrating native Kentucky plants with Japanese garden principles.

Facilities: None

Hours: Daily, sunrise to sunset

Map and self-guided brochure: Can be found on the web site below.

Directions: Follow US 25 (Georgetown Street) north out of Lexington. The gardens are located 0.7 miles north of the Scott County courthouse (the latter being located at the intersection of US 25 and US 460). Alternately, take I-75 north of Lexington to exit #125 (US 460). Turn west (left) on US 460, until reaching US 25. Turn right and travel 0.7 miles. Yuko-En is on your left, adjacent to the Cardome Centre. Park in the small gravel lot on your left.

At the parking lot, the information kiosk will have a variety of news posted, including upcoming events and trail information. However, it's worth bringing those pages you printed off their website so you can sit and read on one of those delectable benches overlooking the koi pond.

According to custom, passing through the Tokugawa Gates releases you from the stresses of everyday life. Bow deeply and leave your western mind behind. You have entered the six-acre Japanese-style stroll garden a la the Bluegrass. Built in 2000 with major funding from Toyota Motor Company and other generous donors, Yuko-En is a sister-city project between Georgetown and Tahara-cho.

The finely graveled path winds through the gardens of Kentucky canebrake, maple trees, and redbud, all intending to emulate traditional Japanese flora. Bearing left, the path leads below the larger of two ponds, to a small waterfall and bridge. Take time to explore. Take time to breathe.

At the top of the hill, the Four Seasons Environmental Education Center (a Japanese style villa) is open for special events, art shows, and performances. Other structures include a 'rake garden,' hermit hut, teahouse, and kiln house. At the far end of the garden, you can also take the path under the US 25 bridge to Cardome Landing, a small park and picnic area along the Elkhorn Creek.

To add a little more mileage and extend your day, take the paved sidewalk away from the parking lot. Just past the small road to the water plant, you'll see signs for the Cardome Walking Trail. The walk is open from 8 am until dusk, and dogs are allowed on leash. Part of an old railroad bed, the trail leads a short distance to the edge of Elkhorn Creek, atop an old stone abutment. Walking the other way, the trail follows the back edge of the Cardome Centre property. Combining Yuko-En and the Cardome Trail, you may have walked a mile.

To add another mile, get back in your car and turn right on US 25, towards Georgetown. Go a few hundred feet and take an immediate left on Payne Avenue, just after crossing Elkhorn Creek. The first left will take you into another small park (you will now be directly across from Cardome Landing). The paved trail runs for almost another mile and is perfect for walking, jogging, and tricycles. The path runs along the Elkhorn Creek in one large loop.

Yuko-En on the Elkhorn
700 Cincinnati Pike (US 25 N)
Georgetown, KY 40324
Phone: (502) 316-4554
Web: yuko-en.com

Part 4
Natural Areas Stewardship

Ethical behavior is doing the right thing
when no one else is watching -
even when doing the wrong thing is legal.
~Aldo Leopold

State Nature Preserves

Natural areas in Kentucky are protected in various ways through federal parks and forests, state parks and forests, county parks, state nature preserves, and by non-profit groups such as The Nature Conservancy.

The following set of rules governing Kentucky's state nature preserves is taken directly from the Kentucky State Nature Preserves Commission. Because this book includes several state nature preserves, we have copied the guidelines verbatim from their website **naturepreserves.ky.gov**.

Rules for State Nature Preserves and State Natural Areas: By observing these rules you will be helping to protect Kentucky's natural heritage.

- Preserves are open sunrise to sunset.
- Trails are open to foot traffic only. The established trail system provides you with the safest and best way to travel through the preserve. Visitors must not re-route or shortcut the existing trail system.
- Horses, bicycles, climbing and rappelling are not permitted in nature preserves because of their destructive impacts to the trails and natural features.
- Motorized vehicles are not permitted.
- Possession of drugs or alcohol is prohibited. Possession of firearms is illegal on dedicated state nature preserves.
- Collecting plants, animals, rocks, artifacts or wood reduces those things that are needed to maintain nature's delicate balance. Therefore, collecting, hunting and trapping are prohibited on dedicated state nature preserves.
- Fishing is allowed only at Metropolis Lake SNP and Six Mile Island SNP.
- Hunting is allowed only at Stone Mountain State Natural Area (SNA), Martin's Fork SNA, Bissell Bluff SNA and Newman's Bluff SNA, in accordance with regulations established by KDFWR under KRS 150 and 300 KAR chapters 1-3.
- To ensure the natural beauty of each preserve and to promote visitor safety and enjoyment, camping, picnicking, building fires, audio equipment and pets are not permitted.
- Remember to carry out your trash.

Rules for state nature preserves are established by 400 KAR 2:090. Any person in violation of this regulation may be liable for a civil penalty of $1,000 per day and possible criminal prosecution as provided for in KRS 224.

Kentucky State Nature Preserves Commission
801 Schenkel Lane
Frankfort, KY 40601
Phone: (502) 573-2886
Web: naturepreserves.ky.gov

The Nature Conservancy

The Nature Conservancy has a similar set of rules as state nature preserves. The following was taken verbatim from their website **nature.org/wherewework/ northamerica/states/kentucky/preserves/art10854.html**

The following activities are permitted on Conservancy preserves:
- Birdwatching
- Hiking
- Nature Study
- Photography
- Boating (in some cases)

What You Cannot Do

Please help us protect our preserves by strictly avoiding the following activities while visiting:
- Bicycling, camping, fires, horseback riding, prospecting, rock climbing, spelunking and swimming.
- Collecting flora, fauna, or mineral specimens, including shells, berries, nuts, mushrooms or wildflowers.
- Using motorized vehicles of any sort except over authorized access roads or buffer zones.
- Fishing, hunting or trapping.
- Pets, including leashed dogs, with the exception of service animals.
- Feeding wildlife.
- Introducing exotic plant or animal species (those that are not native to a particular area).

Respect Our Neighbors' Property

Please do not trespass on private property adjacent to Conservancy preserves. Property lines are clearly marked with small yellow signs featuring the Conservancy's logo.

The Nature Conservancy of Kentucky
642 West Main Street
Lexington, KY 40508
Phone: (859) 259-9655
Web: nature.org/ourinitiatives/regions/northamerica/unitedstates/kentucky

Wildlife Management Areas

Only two Wildlife Management Areas are included in this book (Clay WMA and Kleber WMA). State WMAs are intensively managed by the Kentucky Department of Fish and Wildlife Resources. Their programs include equestrian riding, fish stocking, and a variety of managed hunting seasons. While popular with hunters and fishermen, WMAs also offer limited hiking and biking opportunities for other outdoorsmen and women. A complete list of Kentucky's WMA can be found at **fw.ky.gov/kfwis/viewable/ViewableWMA.asp**.

It is particularly dangerous to be in a Wildlife Management Area during hunting season. We have included the following set of rules that govern WMA use, as taken verbatim from their website **fw.ky.gov/kfwis/wmaguide.asp**. The following rules apply to ALL Wildlife Management Areas owned, leased, or managed by the KDFWR:

1. Area users shall abide by all hunting and fishing laws which apply to the WMA whenever using a WMA for hunting, fishing or trapping.
2. No squirrel, rabbit, quail, grouse, turkey or furbearer hunting or trapping is permitted on WMA's during the first two days of modern gun deer season (second Saturday and Sunday in November), unless the season is open for these species and gun deer hunting is prohibited.
3. WMA visitors shall not enter areas that are closed by signs.
4. Firearms may not be discharged within 100 yards of a residence or occupied building located on or off the WMA. No hunting at any established access point, launching ramp, or recreation area.
5. During a quota deer, pheasant or elk hunt on a WMA, only persons participating in the quota hunt are permitted on the WMA, except waterfowl hunters hunting in some areas posted open.
6. Camping is permitted only in designated areas if such area exists. Campfires are permitted only if attended. No other fires are allowed.
7. Parking must be confined to designated areas if such area exists. If no parking area is designated, parking is generally permitted along maintained roads in such a manner that does not block traffic.
8. Unless otherwise authorized by the KDFWR, vehicles used on WMAs must be street-legal. ATVs and ORVs are not permitted. Vehicles (including motorcycles and bicycles) are permitted only on maintained roads.
9. It is unlawful to cut trees or fences, dump trash or litter, or damage any property or habitat in any fashion. Collecting plants is prohibited.
10. Horseback riding is permitted ONLY on a trail or areas specifically marked for horseback riding or on a maintained public road open to public vehicular traffic, during a permitted event or while engaged in a legal hunting activity.

Kentucky Department of Fish and Wildlife Resources
#1 Sportsman's Lane
Frankfort, KY 40601
Phone: (800) 858-1549
Web: fw.ky.gov/kfwis/viewable/ViewableWMA.asp

Leave No Trace Principles

Widely adopted and respected around the world, leave no trace principles basically assure that we leave nature just as we found it. As our population grows and our natural areas shrink, it is everyone's responsibility to minimize the adverse impact we have on our earth. The guidelines outlined below have been simplified for this book.

- Prepare and plan ahead
    - Bring maps, proper gear, food, and water
- Stay on trails
    - Walk single file in the middle of the trail (unless it is wide such as an old logging road), avoid erosive practices
- Leave rocks, plants, animals, and other artifacts
- Help keep wildlife wild
    - Respect wildlife, particularly during breeding, nesting and birthing seasons
- Respect private property
- Human waste
    - If necessary, dig a 6-8" cat hole at least 200' from water, trails and campsites. Pack out all toilet paper.
- Hike in small groups, use quiet tones, leave music systems at home
- If you packed it in, then pack it out!

Basically this is an updated list combining "Do unto others" with "take only pictures, leave only footprints" philosophies.

For more information, go to the Leave No Trace website at **lnt.org**.

Part 5
You Must Choose...
but Choose Wisely

Most people who travel look only at
what they are directed to look at.
Great is the power of the guidebook maker,
however ignorant.

~John Muir, Travels in Alaska

Trails by Park Amenities

An "*" indicates that the amenity applies unconditionally. A "/" indicates availability under certain conditions.

Bathrooms: Availability may be limited during certain hours. For example, bathrooms may be available when a nature center is open, but not necessarily dawn to dusk. Includes facilities with port-a-potties, as well as those with ceramic tile and soft toilet paper.

Visitors Center: May include nature centers; historical interpretation centers; or historical homes with guided tours.

Pets: An "*" indicates that pets are permitted off leash. A "/" indicates that pets are permitted only if on leash.

Good for Kids: This is a hard one, given the age and interest stratum of those little rugrats. Typically, a trail receives the "good for kids" seal of approval if many of the activities available are specifically targeted for children. Alternately, this tag applies to trails relatively short in duration or a paved trail where kids can bike or skate.

Accessible: Some trails specifically fall into the "paved" category, while other locations do have some paved trail available (but not all of the trails are paved).

Trail Name	Bathrooms	Visitor Center	Pets	Good for Kids	Accessible
Part 1: Hiking Trails					
Asbury Trails at the Palisades Farm			/	*	
Bark Camp Creek			*	*	
Bee Rock and the Rockcastle Narrows	*		*		
Berea College Forest	/		*		
Bernheim Arboretum and Research Forest	*	*	/	*	*
Blue Licks State Nature Preserve	*	*	/	*	
Boone Station State Historic Park	*		/	*	

Trail Name	Bathrooms	Visitor Center	Pets	Good for Kids	Accessible
Buckley Wildlife Sanctuary	*	*		*	
Camp Nelson Civil War Heritage Park	*	*	/	*	
Camp Wildcat	*		/	*	
Capitol View Park	/		/	*	
Carter Caves State Park	*	*	/	*	
Cave Run Lake: Caney Creek Trail Loop	*		*		
Cave Run Lake: Furnace Arch	*		*		
Central Kentucky Wildlife Refuge	*		/	*	
Civil War Fort at Boonesboro			/	*	
Clay WMA/ Marietta Booth Tract			*		
Cove Spring Park and Nature Preserve	*		/	*	
Crutcher Nature Preserve					
Dog Slaughter Falls			*	*	
Dupree Nature Preserve	*			*	
Eagle Falls	*	*		*	
Elkhorn Creek Nature Trail at Great Crossing	*		/	*	
Floracliff Nature Sanctuary	*	*			
Griffith Woods WMA			*	*	
Hisle Park	*		/	*	
Jim Beam Nature Preserve				*	
John A. Kleber Wildlife Management Area			*		

Trail Name	Bathrooms	Visitor Center	Pets	Good for Kids	Accessible
John B. Stephenson Nature Preserve			/		
Leslie Morris Park at Fort Hill	*	*	/	*	*
Lick Creek and Princess Falls			*		
Lower Howard's Creek Nature and Heritage Preserve					
Masterson Station Park	*		/		
Maywoods	/		*		
McConnell Springs	*	*		*	/
Natural Arch Scenic Area	*		*	*	
Natural Bridge: Laurel Ridge Trail Loop	*	*			
Natural Bridge: Rock Garden Trail Loop	*	*			
Perryville Battlefield SP	*	*	/	*	
Pilot Knob State Nature Preserve					
Quiet Trails State Nature Preserve					
Raven Run Nature Sanctuary	*	*		*	/
Red River Gorge: Auxier Ridge/Courthouse Rock Trail Loop	*		*		
Red River Gorge: Rock Bridge/Swift Camp Creek Trail	*		*	*	
Red River Gorge: Sky Bridge Trailapalooza	*	*	*	*	/
Salato Wildlife Education Center	*	*		*	/

Trail Name	Bathrooms	Visitor Center	Pets	Good for Kids	Accessible
Sally Brown Nature Preserve					
Shaker Village: The Nature Preserve	*	*		*	/
Skullbuster: Scott County Adventure Trail			/		
Tom Dorman State Nature Preserve					
Vanhook Falls			*		
Veterans Memorial WMA			*	*	
Veterans Park	*		/	*	/
War Fork Creek	/		*		
Waterfall Chasing: Jackson and Lee Counties	/		/	*	
Yahoo Falls and Arch	*		/	*	
Yahoo Loop via Negro Creek	*		*		
Part 2: Urban Walking Trails					
Frankfort: Capitol Grounds Tour	*	*	/	*	*
Frankfort: Downtown Tour	*		/	*	*
Georgetown: Walk Through Time	*		/	*	*
Lex: African American Heritage Trail			/	*	*
Lex: Historic Lexington Walking Tours			/	*	*
Lexington Walking Tour			/	*	*
LexWalk Audio Tours			/	*	*
Lincoln's Lexington Walking Tour		/	/	*	*
Lexington: Legacy Trail	/		/	*	*

Trail Name	Bathrooms	Visitor Center	Pets	Good for Kids	Accessible
Lexington: Shared and Other Paved Trails			/	*	*
Richmond: Historical / Architectural Tour	*	*	/	*	*
Winchester: Downtown Tour	*		/	*	*
Part 3: Gardens					
The Arboretum, State Botanical Garden of Kentucky	*	*	/	*	*
Ashland: The Henry Clay Estate	*	*	/	*	
Jack Jouett House Historic Site	*	*		*	
Josephine Sculpture Park	*	*		*	
Lexington Cemetery	/		/	*	/
Nannine Clay Wallis Arboretum				*	
Scott County Native Plants Arboretum	*			*	*
Waveland State Historic Site	*	*	/	*	
Woodland Park Tree Trail					
Yuko-En on the Elkhorn and the Cardome Walking Trail				*	

Alphabetical Listing of Trails
with Distance from Lexington and Trail Length

The following list of trails includes information regarding "Distance" (drive time in both the minutes and mileage from downtown Lexington) and "Hiking Trail Mileage" (length of suggested trail, in miles).

Note: Many trails may be easily reduced in length or can be extended for longer hikes. All hikes are measured "round-trip," whether they are loops, out-and-backs, or balloons. Thus, trail mileage includes getting you back to your vehicle again. A '+' indicates that more mileage is readily available.

Trail Name	Distance from Lexington (minutes / miles)	Trail Mileage Options
Part 1: Hiking Trails		
Asbury Trails at the Palisades Farm	33 / 18	2 to 3
Bark Camp Creek	100 / 104	5.2+
Bee Rock and the Rockcastle Narrows	95 / 93	5.4+
Berea College Forest	47 / 43	2.2 to 7.2
Bernheim Arboretum	83 / 75	0.5 to 13.75
Blue Licks State Park Nature Preserve	52 / 41	0.4 to 5
Boone Station State Historic Park	16 / 10	1
Buckley Wildlife Sanctuary	39 / 24	0.3 to 3.3
Camp Nelson Civil War Heritage Park	29 / 20	0.5 to 4
Camp Wildcat Civil War Battlefield	80 / 70	2.5+
Capitol View Park	34 / 25	0.4 to 8
Carter Caves State Park	87 / 92	4.5+
Cave Run Lake: Caney Trail Loop	60 / 59	8.5
Cave Run Lake: Furnace Arch Trail	66 / 62	6
Central Kentucky Wildlife Refuge	68 / 48	0.3 to 6.7
Civil War Fort at Boonesboro	32 / 22	1.4
Clay Wildlife Management Area	54 / 41	2 to 20+
Cove Spring Park and Nature Preserve	31 / 25	0.3 to 6
Crutcher Nature Preserve	40 / 29	2.8 to 5.3

Trail Name	Distance from Lexington (minutes / miles)	Trail Mileage Options
Dog Slaughter Falls	100 / 105	3+
Dupree Nature Preserve	50 / 31	4
Eagle Falls	101 / 105	2.5+
Elkhorn Creek Nature Trail	32 / 15	3
Floracliff Nature Sanctuary	21 / 13	3 to 5
Griffith Woods WMA	33 / 23	1+
Hisle Park	13 / 7	3.5
Jim Beam Nature Preserve	34 / 24	1
John A. Kleber WMA	38 / 28	4.4 to 7.6
John B. Stephenson SNP	59 / 50	2
Leslie Morris Park at Fort Hill	33 / 24	0.6 to 4.8
Lick Creek and Princess Falls	109 / 112	8
Lower Howard's Creek Nature Preserve	25 / 17	5+
Masterson Station Park	8 / 3	4.5
Maywoods	54 / 53	1 to 6
McConnell Springs	5 / 2	0.25 to 2
Natural Arch Scenic Area	108 / 103	8
Natural Bridge State Park: Laurel Ridge Trail Loop	56 / 57	3.5
Natural Bridge State Park: Rock Garden Trail Loop	56 / 57	3.25
Perryville Battlefield State Historic Site	69 / 45	1 to 10.5
Pilot Knob State Nature Preserve	43 / 42	0.8 to 7
Quiet Trails State Nature Preserve	56 / 41	3.1
Raven Run Nature Sanctuary	16 / 8	2 to 10
Red River Gorge: Auxier Ridge/Courthouse Rock Trail Loop	67 / 62	5.2
Red River Gorge: Rock Bridge and Swift Camp Creek Trail	70 / 68	1.4 to 10.5
Red River Gorge: Sky Bridge Trailapalooza	72 / 70	2
Salato Wildlife Education Center	34 / 25	0.5 to 3.5
Sally Brown Nature Preserve	40 / 29	2.5 to 5.3

Trail Name	Distance from Lexington (minutes / miles)	Trail Mileage Options
Shaker Village: The Nature Preserve	34 / 24	1 to 6+
Skullbuster: Scott Co. Adventure Trails	38 / 24	7.8
Tom Dorman State Nature Preserve	35 / 24	1.9 to 2.6
Vanhook Falls	90 / 89	5.4
Veterans Memorial WMA	30 / 22	.5+
Veterans Park	13 / 6	3.4
War Fork Creek / Resurgence Cave	100 / 65	5
Waterfall Chasing: Jackson and Lee Counties	115 / 78	3
Yahoo Falls and Yahoo Arch	127 / 109	2+
Yahoo Loop via Negro Creek	128 / 110	9.5+
Part 2: Urban Walking Trails		
Frankfort: Capitol Grounds Walking Tour	40 / 25	1.25
Frankfort: Downtown Walking Tour	40 / 25	1.5
Georgetown: Walk Through Time	27 / 13	2
Lex: African American Heritage Trail	0 / 0	3.25 to 4
Historic Lexington Walking Tour: Adaptive Reuse Walking Tour	0 / 0	0.5
Historic Lexington Walking Tour: Constitution Historic District	0 / 0	0.5
Historic Lexington Walking Tour: Gratz Park	0 / 0	0.5
Historic Lexington Walking Tour: Mulberry Hill	0 / 0	0.5
Lexington Walk	0 / 0	2
LexWalk Audio Tour	0 / 0	2
Lincoln's Lexington Walking Tour	0 /0	2.5
Lexington Legacy Trail	5 / .5	1 to 17
Lex: Shared Use and Other Paved Trails	varies	0.5 to 2.5 each
Richmond: Historical and Architectural Walking Tour	8 / 25	2
Winchester: Downtown Walking Tour	30 / 20	1.5

Trail Name	Distance from Lexington (minutes / miles)	Trail Mileage Options
Part 3: Gardens		
The Arboretum, State Botanical Garden of Kentucky	5 / 2	0.25 to 2+
Ashland: The Henry Clay Estate	4 / 2	1.0
Jack Jouett House Historic Site	33 / 19	0.25
Josephine Sculpture Park	42 / 31	0.5
Lexington Cemetery	1 / .5	2.5
Nannine Clay Wallis Arboretum	24 /18	.25
Scott County Native Plants Arboretum	20 / 12	.25
Waveland State Historic Site	15 / 6	1
Woodland Park Tree Trail	3 / 0.8	0.5
Yuko-En on the Elkhorn and the Cardome Walking Trail	20 / 13	1

Index

About the Author

After spending more than 20 years as a university researcher and professor, Valerie traded the ivory towers of academia for the great outdoors. Her background in natural resource economics and love of nature translated into a

second career of writing outdoor guides, including "Hike the Bluegrass", "Five Star Trails: Louisville and Southern Indiana", and "Fly Fishing Kentucky". An avid outdoorswoman, Valerie has swum in Africa's Lake Malawi, climbed China's Mount Tai, sailed the coast of southern France, biked Nova Scotia, and backpacked the überchallenging West Coast Trail of Vancouver Island. Her honeymoon was spent kayaking the Grand Canyon with her husband, Ben. The mother of four, Valerie lives in Lexington, Kentucky and hits the trail every chance she gets.

Photo by Emma Askren

Other books of interest

CPSIA information can be obtained
at www.ICGtesting.com
Printed in the USA
BVHW060756141218
535597BV00010B/110/P